The Fall of Northern Rock

An insider's story of Britain's biggest banking disaster

by

Brian Walters

HARRIMAN HOUSE LTD

3A Penns Road
Petersfield
Hampshire
GU32 2EW
GREAT BRITAIN

Tel: +44 (0)1730 233870
Fax: +44 (0)1730 233880
Email: enquiries@harriman-house.com
Website: www.harriman-house.com

First published in Great Britain in 2008
Copyright © Harriman House Ltd

The right of Brian Walters to be identified as author has been asserted
in accordance with the Copyright, Design and Patents Acts 1988.

ISBN 13: 978-1905641-80-2

British Library Cataloguing in Publication Data
A CIP catalogue record for this book can be obtained from the British Library.

Printed and bound by the CPI Group, Antony Rowe, Chippenham.

Contents

Contents

About the Author

Brian Walters has worked in the banking industry for 36 years, having started his career at Barclays in 1971, moved up to the role of Corporate Manager in Coventry in 1992, and then moved to Leeds in 1999 as Head of Small Business for West Yorkshire.

He joined Northern Rock in 2005 to manage the Yorkshire based Commercial Finance Division and was there throughout the turmoil of 2007, but left in early 2008 to join a major building society as a Senior Lending Manager with its Commercial Division.

Brian lives in Harrogate with his wife and family.

"2007 was a difficult and challenging year for Northern Rock"

Northern Rock Annual Report, 2007

Introduction

In writing the introduction to this book about the Northern Rock crash, I am drawn to a recent article in *The Spectator* entitled "A Crash to Remember". This article talks about how financial markets are human in nature, and that anything that goes wrong in them is almost certain to have happened before and highly likely to happen again. It goes on to say that money muddles always start the same way – when judgement is fuddled by greed, ambition and overwhelming self-confidence. Then, when problems arise, there follows an obstinate refusal to admit mistakes or the imminence of disaster.

This article, however, was not about the Northern Rock crash; it was dated 30th September 2006, almost a year before that disaster. It was instead about the failure in 1866 of Overend, Gurney & Co, which was the last UK bank, prior to Northern Rock, to have had a run on it.

Overend, Gurney & Co was a respected bank that for a number of years was the greatest discounting-house in the world. Its problems arose when it took on substantial investments in long-term investments, such as railways, rather than holding short-term cash reserves as was necessary for its role. Eventually it found itself with liabilities of around £4 million, and liquid assets of only £1 million, at which point it requested assistance from the Bank of England. This was refused and the following day panic spread across the City of London, with large crowds gathered around its offices at 65 Lombard Street.[1]

It is easy, in hindsight, to see a similarity between the two events; but 141 years is a long time and it is quite astounding to think that this length of time passed before crowds of people were again on the streets desperate to withdraw their cash from a UK bank. The difference is that in 1866 live television pictures of the event were not broadcast around the world.

Coincidentally, in 1865 – at a time when Overend & Gurney was desperately trying to shore up its capital base – the Rock Building Society was founded. One hundred years later, in 1965, it merged with the Northern Counties Permanent Benefit and Investment Building Society to become the Northern Rock Building Society.

Over the following forty years Northern Rock flourished and became, by the time I joined it in 2005, one of the most highly respected and envied financial institutions in the UK.

I have been involved in the banking industry for all my working life which is, I might add, quite a long time – 36 years at the last count. During that time I have seen a number of stock market declines, a major recession, three banks fail (Johnson Matthey, Barings and BCCI), property crashes, the dot com boom and bust, and numerous other financial disasters. However, the Northern Rock collapse, which started on 14th September 2007 with the run on the bank and culminated in it being taken into public ownership on 18th February 2008, is probably the most spectacular disaster of all.

It was so spectacular because of the sheer scale of its fall from grace. Such a highly successful and profitable company – the largest private sector employer in the north-east, a high-profile sponsor of Newcastle United Football Club and, at its peak, the

---

[1] For further information on Overend & Gurney see *The Mystery of Overend & Gurney: Financial Scandal in Victorian London* (Methuen, 2006)

fifth largest mortgage lender in the UK – was rendered almost worthless in just a few short months and taken into public ownership supported by the Bank of England to the tune of a reported £100 billion in loans and guarantees.

Northern Rock will now only ever be remembered for the pictures beamed around the world of long, snaking queues of people outside its branches desperate to withdraw their savings.

But that is not how I remember Northern Rock, because I worked for it during some very good times.

I was there, as an employee, before, during and after the run and, given that the last run on a UK bank was in 1866, I feel that to work for a company going though this type of crisis is a rare thing indeed – and certainly a story worth telling.

So telling the story is what I do in this book. It is not my intention to provide sensational revelations or indeed run down an organisation that for the vast majority of its life was extremely successful and a very good employer. It is more to recount my personal experiences at Northern Rock before, during and after the crisis, whilst commenting on the events that unfolded around me and what impact they had on the business and the people within it.

I also want to explore the whole background to the fall of Northern Rock, explain what I think caused it, how it could possibly have been avoided, and to document the chain of events that led to the final conclusion which is, of course, its eventual nationalisation.

If there is to be anything positive to come out of the fall of Northern Rock it will, in my view, be in the lessons to be learnt from the events that led up to it. Examples of such lessons are the financial risks attached to rapid growth in a business, the importance of cash to a business, the role played by regulatory bodies in protecting the consumer and controlling the banking industry, the impact on people when confidence in a bank evaporates, the power of the media in influencing events and, finally, ensuring that there is a robust mechanism in place to deal quickly and effectively with a major banking crisis should one ever happen again.

The Northern Rock collapse will attract debate for years to come and everyone will have their own opinion about it. For what it is worth this is mine.

Starting at the Rock

When I started at Northern Rock I am sure that I went through the same emotions as anybody starting with a new employer. It is rather like going to a new school and all the real but often unfounded fears that tend to go with that.

The people I would be working with I had already met, but meeting someone and working with them are two rather different things. My role was to manage Northern Rock's commercial finance office in Leeds which was, and still is, located on the 5th floor of a large office building in the centre of Leeds.

Having spent many years with Barclays I noticed an immediate difference from the rather intense sales environment of a major bank. People within Northern Rock seemed more relaxed, less stressed and seemed to have a real affection for the organisation. My immediate feeling was that the organisation treated its staff well and, whilst there certainly was an expectation that results had to be delivered, there was an understanding that instant results were not always possible. Providing that one was moving in the right direction the company was generally very supportive.

As I think most people do when they start a new job, the first few weeks are spent observing what is going on, who does what, trying to understand new systems and trying to get a feel for the organisation as a whole.

I spent my first few days at the Leeds office getting to understand how its business was conducted and how to operate the various systems attached to my role. I was not used to working with such a small team but having come from the pressure cooker environment of a major bank where, frankly, there is enormous stress on customer-facing staff to sell the bank's products, I found this new environment to be rather a refreshing change.

During the second week I spent a couple of days attending a hastily put together induction programme which had only just been designed for the benefit of myself and two colleagues based in Edinburgh and St. Albans who had both joined at roughly the same time. There had been no formal induction plan previously and this event had been designed to give us a complete overview of our roles. The event also involved us meeting, on day two, all the key people we would be dealing with at Northern Rock's Commercial Finance Head Office in Doxford Park, Sunderland. Within this building were the underwriting, case management and administration teams, together with the various monitoring and control functions that dealt with such things as loan reviews and arrears.

Our role in the offices was to sell loans and get the cases agreed by the underwriters. The legal work behind the loans was undertaken by external solicitors and approved by Northern Rock's case management team, who were then responsible for the eventual release of funds.

Whilst there were some frictions, I quickly found I regarded these as being the same as those that exist in most banks and building societies. These were, for instance, underwriters being slow to recognise the merits of a lending proposal, head office not sharing our sense of emergency in trying to ensure that funds were released on time for a property purchase, and an obsession by the organisation as a whole to maintain a tight rein on expenditure.

A Geordie welcome

Whilst everyone will always try to create a good first impression, I found everyone I came into contact with at Northern Rock extremely helpful, and I can only put that down to the people of the north-east themselves. From my experience, they are some of the most genuine, down-to-earth people I have ever met. It was impossible to work for Northern Rock and not have a very strong feel for its north-east roots; after all, almost everyone you came into contact with had a Geordie accent!

Northern Rock also struck me as a very paternal organisation that looked after its staff. Everyone I met was approachable, helpful and appreciative of the company, with many having worked for it since leaving school. There were many examples of staff who had worked their way up to senior positions within Northern Rock, never having worked for anybody else. Perhaps the highest profile example of this was Adam Applegarth, Northern Rock's chief executive, who had started with Northern Rock as a new entrant in 1983.

Back at the office in Leeds I was still feeling my way. It was like going back in time to the sort of working environment I had experienced twenty-five years previously. At that time, I was based in the office with a stand-alone computer and a secretary who answered the phone, kept files up to date and did audio typing.

This added to the appeal of my new job. It was like going back to being an old-fashioned bank manager again. The important thing was, however, to understand that this was quite an unusual set up for a business in the new millennium, so the key was to enjoy it whilst it lasted.

Speaking of keys, I noticed something rather peculiar about the keyboard to my computer in that when I pressed the £ key it printed #. I concluded that this might prove to be something of a handicap when compiling lending reports. Indeed, if there was any one particular symbol that was an absolute necessity for someone in a bank lending role it was that one, yet it was the one symbol my keyboard would not produce. I had no trouble with the dollar sign. This took weeks to resolve.

I found this quite amusing, indeed quirky, and the fact that I was writing reports for three weeks without using the pound sign didn't seem to bother anyone. Yes, these were really laid-back people!

It might be useful at this stage to look briefly at the history of the bank I had just joined.

A Short History of Northern Rock

As mentioned in the introduction the roots of Northern Rock can be traced back to 1865, but its recent history started exactly one hundred years later, in 1965.

Northern Rock, as we know it today, started its life on 8th July 1965, as the result of the merger of two existing Newcastle-based building societies. These were the Northern Counties Permanent Benefit and Investment Building Society (originally formed in 1850) and the Rock Building Society (originally formed in 1865). The abbreviated "Northern Rock Building Society" became the name of the combined building societies, and whilst it was by far the largest building society in Newcastle it was a minnow, at that time, compared with, say, the Halifax, which was fourteen times larger. Northern Rock in 1965 was number sixteen in the building society rankings.

Northern Rock then grew mainly by making acquisitions starting initially, in 1966, with the Workington Permanent Building Society and then, between 1971 and 1981, by taking over a further twenty-two building societies. Between 1979 and 1983, the society's assets doubled from £500 million to £1,000 million – partly through acquisitions and partly through organic growth.

It was in 1990 that Northern Rock started to diversify into commercial lending and that was when its commercial finance division was started.

Over the next few years Northern Rock continued to expand by around 15% per annum and, because of its low exposure to property in the South (where falls in property values were deepest) it emerged relatively unscathed from the recession in the early 1990s. The results for the first nine months of 1993 revealed the best figures ever, with assets up 16.4% to over £7,000 million and profits in excess of the previous years' with still three months left to run.

In 1994, after unsuccessful merger talks in previous years with both the Britannia and Birmingham Midshires building societies, Northern Rock acquired the Sunderland based North of England Building Society. This was a major acquisition with 300,000 investment accounts, 43,000 borrowers and assets of over £1,500 million. This gave Northern Rock the size and the financial muscle it was seeking. It also made Northern Rock a top ten player with assets exceeding £10 billion. Over four years it had increased its size threefold, its profits fourfold and had halved its management expense ratios.

Northern Rock demutualises and becomes a public company

However, in the mid 1990s, high-profile takeovers such as that of Cheltenham and Gloucester by Lloyds Bank and the acquisition of the Leeds Building Society by the Halifax, left Northern Rock feeling vulnerable to an approach by a predator. In 1995, the idea of converting to PLC status was discussed and on 19th December 1995 the proposal to convert was formally put to the board.

Chris Sharp was Chief Executive at the time and Robert Dickinson the Chairman. The proposal included the idea that 15% of the issued share capital of the new PLC and 5% of its annual profit should be used to set up a charitable foundation to support good causes, principally in the north-east. This charity, called the Northern Rock Foundation, is still in place today and the company took great pride in giving something back to various good causes in the north-east from the profits it made.

The climax of the conversion exercise came at a special general meeting on 15th April 1997, when it was confirmed that Northern Rock would cease to be a building society on 1st October 1997.

The transformation of Northern Rock into a public company was a huge success. The shares were three times oversubscribed at £4.50 each. All qualifying members received a windfall of 500 shares each – worth £2,250 at that time. Its demutualisation meant that Northern Rock was no longer a building society effectively owned by its members. Instead, it was now a bank owned by its shareholders.

Sadly, Chris Sharp was never to see this day because he died of a heart attack on 8th May 1997, having led the building society over the previous fifteen years. Leon Finn replaced him as Chief Executive and in the year 2001, he was succeeded by Adam Applegarth.

The rate of growth continued strongly. In the year ended 31st December 2000, the company made a pre-tax profit of £250 million, and by 2005 this had almost doubled to £494 million, representing an annualised growth rate of 20% – an impressive performance indeed.

Although Northern Rock was described as a bank it did not provide the full range of services that, say, Barclays would provide. Its main products were residential mortgages and buy to lets, savings accounts, commercial mortgages and unsecured personal loans. But it did extremely well in these markets by competing very aggressively on price. Northern Rock almost always featured in the "best buy" columns of the Sunday papers and its success was envied by its competitors.

How did it achieve such success?

There were a number of factors that helped Northern Rock grow so strongly:

It had managed to retain its independence in an environment where many other building societies had been taken over. Indeed, it had grown its business by making a number of acquisitions of its own.

It had taken advantage of demutualisation, through which it was able to raise additional capital to accelerate its growth further.

Its cost base was the lowest in the industry, which enabled it to be extremely competitive.

It focused on the areas it was good at, so that it was highly successful in the markets it was active in.

Its product range was innovative and highly competitive.

Finally, it had an ambitious management with a game plan for Northern Rock to become one of the major mortgage lenders in the UK.

Just before I started at Northern Rock its share price had reached £8.00. Those investors who bought in to the floatation of Northern Rock as a PLC had seen their investment almost double.

A well run business

There was no question that here was an extremely well run business that was punching well above its weight and one which was admired by the financial analysts in the City. Not only that, it was liked by its customers, respected by its competitors and by and large seen by its staff as an excellent employer.

The Commercial Finance Division

Northern Rock's commercial finance business

I should explain at this stage what type of business Northern Rock Commercial Finance actually did, what type of loans it made on what sort of terms and to which type of borrowers.

Northern Rock's commercial finance business was conducted through eight small, strategically located local teams of specialist lending managers and support staff. These offices were located in Bristol, Bromley, St. Albans, Birmingham, Manchester, Leeds, Newcastle and Edinburgh.

Its strategy was to lend selectively to what were considered to be low-risk sectors, such as professional buy to let landlords, commercial property investors, professional practices (accountants, doctors' surgeries, etc.) and the residential healthcare market (e.g. nursing and residential care homes). Historically, these types of businesses, which were mainly property based, had offered more resilience in the face of an economic downturn than other types of businesses, such as pubs, hotels, or manufacturing.

In terms of the types of customers Northern Rock did business with, these were generally residential and commercial property investors who were keen to build a portfolio of properties to rent out. The key principle being that the rent would cover the loan repayments. Over a period of years the expectation was that both the rental income and capital values relating to the properties would increase and that would enable Northern Rock to provide further funding against the portfolio to buy further properties. At the time this was considered to be a much more flexible approach to that offered by the major banks, who were not so keen to "gear up" (as it is described), to the increasing value of the lender's security (i.e. the properties being lent against).

Commercial loans with Northern Rock started at £250,000 and went up to as much as £75 million. Above that level, exposure to one single borrower was considered a potential risk so this was pretty much the single customer exposure limit. Potentially this was sizeable business being conducted through a small team of people. In reality the larger offices (e.g. Manchester and St. Albans) did the bigger ticket loans because of the major broker contacts they had. Leeds office had only five staff but nevertheless it had a few borrowers with property portfolios of just below the £20 million mark, so there was some sizeable business there.

Generally, this was long-term finance to borrowers who had acquired properties to rent out. On the residential side, these properties ranged from domestic houses forming part of a buy to let portfolio, larger blocks of apartments, and student properties including apartment blocks. On the commercial property side, we lent to landlords or property companies who owned industrial units, retail shops and office buildings primarily, and who had rented these out.

It was an interesting business to be in. Certainly far more diverse than the more standard residential mortgage business with which Northern Rock was more commonly associated.

Commercial finance was not a major part of Northern Rock's business; it probably accounted for about 3% of its overall mortgages and profit. Some of this was due to the commercial business not having grown as quickly as it perhaps should have done, and some of it due to the extraordinary growth in the company's residential mortgage business, which had simply outpaced the more sluggish growth on the commercial side.

I was concerned that being such a small element of its overall business was a potential disadvantage, but I was assured that its commercial business was very much valued by the board and was considered an important part of the company's overall business. It was also highly profitable.

Our office

The commercial finance office was located away from the local branch, and within it was a small team of two lending managers and two support staff, all female.

The office had clearly gone through a fair degree of trauma prior to my arrival. My predecessor, who had been there for over four years, had left in January to join a commercial finance brokerage and it had taken four months to replace him. It had also taken roughly the same amount of time to bring in a new support manager.

The office had therefore done little for much of the first few months of 2005, and levels of new business were fairly low. My arrival, together with the fact that we now had a new team together, was expected to be the springboard needed to get the Leeds office onto the map.

Whilst at this stage I knew little about Northern Rock and therefore needed to understand the culture, the systems and how the business worked, I was very much looking forward to the challenge.

Good old-fashioned relationship banking

I was amazed to discover that as a commercial business within Northern Rock there were no cross sale targets. None at all. Cross sales is an expression to describe a situation where on the back of providing a loan, for instance, one tries to achieve other sales for the company such as property insurance, life insurance, deposits, income protection cover – the list is endless. I am quite open to the concept of introducing value adding products to any transaction, provided that they are relevant, competitive and meet the customer's needs, however this was simply not something that Northern Rock did. The emphasis was purely on securing the loan deal and making sure that the borrower did the transaction through Northern Rock. This made life very simple for all concerned even though, I suspected, there might be some lost opportunities attached to this strategy.

In terms of the way Northern Rock conducted its business in commercial finance it seemed to me a throw back to – what is often described as – good old-fashioned relationship banking. Meetings with customers were generally relaxed, constructive and focused almost entirely on putting the funding in place to enable them to purchase or refinance the particular property or properties they were seeking. I liked it; simple, uncomplicated and generally – because most of the people I dealt with were very experienced property investors who understood their market – an absolute pleasure to deal with.

A reason Northern Rock was attractive to them was that it was very simple and straightforward to deal with. But the major attraction was that lending margins on commercial loans were extremely competitive at between 1% and 1.25% for the better quality deals. These margins had come down significantly from where they had been just a couple of years previously, due to a combination of low interest rates, increasing competition between lenders and a stable economic climate.

Because Northern Rock had such a low cost base and a low default history it was able to compete with other lenders who had a wider spread of activity.

Whilst this sort of margin seems very low, these were substantial deals so, a £5 million loan, for instance, would produce a gross income of £75,000 for Northern Rock in the first year.

The state of the business

The systems I found in commercial finance were quite different to those on the residential side of the business, which were far more streamlined. It was difficult to find out basic information like how much we were lending as an office. This information could be provided by Head Office, on request, but wasn't readily accessible through our office computer system.

After making an appropriate request to Head Office I was e-mailed a customer list showing that the office had about 250 borrowers with a combined exposure of around £310 million, so there was a reasonable business. However, within the office we did not have a detailed customer list or any sort of system to plan and manage those relationships. Indeed, we had many customers who, as a business, we had simply lost contact with. If a business loses contact with its existing customers and has no strategy to rectify that with a view to developing and strengthening the relationships, there is not a lot of point in devoting one's time to finding new business. Indeed, prospecting far and wide for diamonds is pointless when many of the diamonds you need are already in your own backyard.

Some of these things I considered as quirky, but on reflection this was not so much quirkiness but more a failure to get some of the basic things right. I felt that the potential to grow the business was enormous, but first of all I needed to understand who our customers were and what potential there might be to grow these relationships.

Each commercial finance office was targeted to achieve a certain level of new lending business each year. The size of the target depended on a number of factors including historical performance, the perceived level of opportunity and the number of lending managers operating in the team. In 2005, the property market was buoyant and expectations were high.

The property market at the time

Economic conditions had been stable for a number of years and interest rates were low, at 4.75%. This had led to property (both residential and commercial) enjoying considerable growth; on average the annual average growth returns on property were in the order of 12%. The demand for borrowed money was high because investors could see an opportunity to increase their wealth through buying property. Not only did they expect their income to grow as rents increased, but they could also expect to see the value of their properties increase.

Because there was an increasing and seemingly infinite demand for property from investors, this in turn led to more lenders getting into the commercial property market and so competition between lenders exploded. This led to several things happening. Firstly, borrowers had more providers to choose from and were therefore in a strong position to demand higher levels of funding from lenders and at increasingly lower rates. The increasing demand for property was starting to lead to properties being sold at auction for increasingly inflated prices. This in turn meant that the returns to investors from property investment were starting to decrease because rent rises were not keeping pace with property value increases. However, they were still buying because many of them believed that even if the income returns were relatively low they would make their gains from the capital appreciation of the properties.

How to become a millionaire in five years

By way of illustration, Northern Rock had buy to let borrowers who had each bought ten properties in the year 2000 at £100,000 each and had borrowed 85% of their value. That meant that they had put in a £150,000 deposit and borrowed £850,000 to acquire properties worth £1,000,000. Within five years the value of these properties had almost doubled, the loan was at the same level with rent having covered the interest. The properties were now worth

£200,000 each, making a total of £2,000,000. They had become paper millionaires in five years for a £150,000 deposit.

In 2005, within our office in Leeds we had a number of borrowers who had done this and were now sitting on properties bought five years previously that had almost doubled in value since then. Most of the investment had been provided through a Northern Rock loan. However, the market had been remarkably kind to property investors over this time because interest rates had been low and demand for property high.

Obviously these sort of conditions do not last forever, but in 2005 the market was red hot and showed no sign of abating.

A target of one hundred million pounds

In 2005, Northern Rock Commercial Finance, as a business, was targeted to bring in £1 billion of new commercial lending to the business. I was expected to deliver a tenth of that, £100 million, through my office in Leeds. When I arrived in May the office was achieving new business levels of roughly half that figure and was ranked 5th out of the eight offices across the UK.

Some of this had been due to almost constant under-resourcing in the various offices which, I hasten to add, was not a deliberate policy but more as a result of the extraordinary demand for staff in the commercial lending market.

For instance, it had taken several months to recruit both myself and a new assistant, whose role it was to free the lending managers up from dealing with administrative queries. During that time the two female managers in place were only really able to tread water. This naturally led to the temporary underperformance of the Leeds office.

However, with the staffing problems solved, the first few weeks were full of optimism. There was now a new, well resourced team in place with every opportunity to do well.

Not a Good Start

Headhunters circling

Within three weeks of starting with Northern Rock a strange thing happened. I had a call from a search and selection consultant who asked if I would be interested in an opportunity to work for a building society that was looking to increase its presence in the commercial property finance market in Leeds. I explained that I had only just started my role with Northern Rock but was interested to know how he had managed to get hold of my name. What he said surprised me, which was that Northern Rock was the first place he, and others, went to when recruiting for other companies. That was because it was recognised as having quality staff who were, by and large, being paid below the industry average.

Two weeks later I had a similar call from another headhunter, this time calling on behalf of an Irish based bank looking for a commercial lending manager for its Leeds based commercial property team. Again, I declined to take this further.

What this was telling me though was that potentially Northern Rock had a problem in retaining its staff. Property lending was a massive growth industry at that time and most banks were either trying to set up new teams in Leeds or expanding existing teams. This was also the case everywhere else in the UK. Since this was a specialised area where the skills involved were fairly rare and in high demand this was a real threat to its business.

Northern Rock staff were generally extremely loyal and what I quickly came to realise was that the type of calls I had received most people were getting on a regular basis, and whilst most approaches were resisted because the staff approached took the view that the grass is not always greener on the other side, the company, in my view, could not continue to rely on its employees' loyalty for ever.

Northern Rock had a reputation for training their managers well, so their employees were generally of high quality and thus in great demand in the employment market. What did not help, in my view, was that salary scales were constrained by a fairly rigid framework called the "career pathway". This was well intentioned, in that it was a very fair and visible reward system that enabled staff to progress within their jobs to certain levels and, under normal circumstances, would have been absolutely fine. However, there was a cap to the maximum salary that could be paid for any specific role, and therefore in a highly competitive market this restricted the rate at which strong performers could be rewarded. This was to become an increasing problem for Commercial Finance, but what the company clearly was not prepared to do was to compromise its reward system for what was a relatively small part of its business. It was a difficult conundrum at the time.

The first couple of months went quickly and I had, by this time, got a grasp of Northern Rock's lending criteria and had drawn up plans to increase the profile of Northern Rock in the market place. Despite the fact that Northern Rock was an extremely well known name, very few people, even those in the commercial finance industry, knew that it did buy to let portfolios and commercial property finance. There were, therefore, huge opportunities in the market that were being lost simply because we had not got in front of enough people to tell them about the type of lending we did.

I suppose what c oncerned me more was that the people who worked for Northern Rock locally, on the residential side of the business, did not know what we did either, so there was a big PR job to be done in getting the right message across. Initial discussions with them indicated that there were real opportunities for us to work closer together, but before I had a chance to put any of these plans into action my office underwent the sort of upheaval that made any previous resourcing problems look like a walk in the park.

Staff leaving

The team I inherited had been loyal to Northern Rock and had worked for the company, on average, for about three years. They were by and large happy with the company, apart from the usual irritations, but it became clear fairly early on that the prospect of working for another company for an improved financial package was something they would consider.

So it was not a great surprise when one of my managers announced that she had obtained an opportunity elsewhere on a higher salary and had decided to leave. She was put on immediate gardening leave and I took over dealing with her accounts. Then, three weeks later, my Area Director also resigned, to take up a position with a large firm of commercial finance brokers.

I couldn't believe it. My first few months with Northern Rock had turned out to be a baptism of fire.

I should perhaps have suspected something when the two other people on my induction course were both senior commercial finance managers starting on roughly the same day. In other words, three out of the eight commercial finance offices of Northern Rock had only just filled vacancies for their most senior role. I knew now why their predecessors had left – attractive salary packages offered by other lenders in a mature market had proved to be too much of a temptation.

There was certainly a shortage of good quality commercial lending managers in the market as a result of an increasing number of lenders having gone into the commercial loan market, Abbey and Alliance & Leicester being two good examples.

But it got worse.

Within two months, and before I had a replacement in place for the manager who had left, both the remaining manager and assistant also handed in their notices and left Northern Rock to join competitors. By October I had lost all of my team except for a clerical assistant – who was on long-term sick leave following an operation. I was now in the position where I was running the business on my own, with a temp, and a target of £100 million.

Looking back on the chain of events there were plenty of clues that this sort of thing might happen. Sometimes, when one inherits a team of managers one instinctively knows whether they are going to be fully on board or not with what you are trying to achieve. Whilst I thought that, in time, I could create that sense of collective enthusiasm and ambition to succeed, any plans to do this were overtaken by events.

However, it really was the case that both of my colleagues at that time had an opportunity to move on to what they thought was a better opportunity and they took it.

A matter of rebuilding the unit

At this point I was given the fullest support by my immediate managers, particularly my newly appointed Area Director who drafted in experienced staff from other areas of the business (Manchester and Newcastle) to support me. My new Area Director had previously undertaken my role at Northern Rock's Newcastle commercial office and had designed the induction programme I had attended when I first joined. She was very much a people person and was extremely supportive in the rebuilding of the Leeds office. The staff who were drafted in from other offices were also tremendously helpful. What struck me – and I haven't seen this in many organisations – was the willingness to spend time doing things that contributed nothing towards their own targets or objectives. It was a real pleasure to experience some honest team working.

As 2005 drew to a close I knew that I had to embark on a major rebuilding process. The office lent £47 million in new loans that year, way below the office target but, in the circumstances, this was probably not a bad performance. I had lent very little personally at that stage but I had ensured, as best as I could, that I had personally contacted all of our key customers to explain the position and to keep them on board.

I now had to rebuild the team and it was so important that I recruited well. Northern Rock's business was booming elsewhere and what I clearly had to do was put 2005 behind me and rebuild the business in 2006.

This had certainly been a torrid first six months in my new career with Northern Rock.

Going for Growth

Stellar growth

Despite the problems I'd been having in the Leeds office, the 2005 annual results for Northern Rock were impressive. Record profits of £308 million (an increase of 14% over 2004), and underlying net assets of £81.1 billion (an increase of 25%). The company also achieved record net lending of £14.6 billion (an increase of 12.6% on 2004) and a ratio of costs to assets of 0.34% – the best in the industry.

In addition, Adam Applegarth reported that during 2005 there had been a significant investment in people, systems and premises to support increased business volumes. As well as the expansion of Northern Rock's headquarters at Gosforth, the development of a new office complex at Rainton Bridge in Sunderland was announced, with potential for up to 2,500 new jobs.

So, all round, busy, busy, busy.

In researching this chapter the following piece caught my eye:

> *Northern Rock has been revitalized. We have returned to rapid growth. This is clearly demonstrated in our first half results with all areas of the business performing strongly.*

*We are one of the fastest growing mortgage lenders in the
UK. We have the lowest costs. By integrating e-commerce
across the business we support growth and cost efficiency.*

*We are focused, innovative, consumer friendly, and deliver
on our promises. Northern Rock is unique in its sector and
there is a growing recognition in our achievements.*

Stirring stuff. The piece was actually written in July 2000 by Leo
Finn, the former chief executive and the predecessor of Adam
Applegarth. The fact is nothing really changed when Applegarth
became chief executive – "going for growth" was very much
business as usual. But possibly the difference was in the speed and
intensity with which the growth was delivered.

The Virtuous Cycle

In 2005, 45% of the UK mortgage market represented
remortgages. This is where mortgage customers of other lenders
come to the end of their initial fixed rate deal and are in a position
to shop round for a better deal from another lender. Northern
Rock had considerable success in attracting a good proportion of
these borrowers by offering very competitive deals.

Its business model at the time was called "The Virtuous Cycle".
Within this cycle there were three components: cost control,
competitive and innovative products, and high quality asset growth.
The rationale behind this was that by operating a low cost and
efficient business it could offer competitive and innovative products
which would attract more customers and lead to more growth.

The question was how was this growth to be funded?

Northern Rock's funding strategy

To the staff of Northern Rock, and in particular to those who were
engaged in lending Northern Rock's money to the customer, it was
a "given" that the funds were available to lend. We did not pay any
attention to where the funds came from. This was the function of

Northern Rock's head office treasury function to sort out. And over a 40 year period they seemed to have managed that without any problem – so why should that change?

Funding a growing mortgage book is a fairly complex process to describe, but it was Northern Rock's ability to do this successfully that had been the cornerstone of its success.

What, however, separated Northern Rock from most banks and building societies is that they had a relatively low level of retail deposits. Whilst Northern Rock did offer competitive savings products through a number of channels – such as internet and postal accounts – its presence in the High Street was fairly slim, in that it only had 76 branches in the UK.

The problem was that its loans were growing faster than its deposits.

Many years ago this fact alone would have severely handicapped Northern Rock's ability to grow its business, because due to banking regulations banks could only lend a proportion of the deposits they held and, clearly, if a bank could not grow its deposits it could not grow its loans either.

But over the years this had changed. Put simply, whilst the overall capital requirements for each bank are tightly regulated, there was no longer a requirement for significant levels of deposits to be held to support a bank's lending activities.

So banks are now allowed to lend substantially more than the amount of deposits it holds. As a rough figure, this would be around six times the amount of its deposits.

But Northern Rock went further than this.

It had found that there was a healthy market for its mortgages from institutional investors. So what Northern Rock did was to bundle some of its mortgages together and sell the future revenue income stream to them. They did this through a separate offshore company called Granite – this process was called "securitisation".

The process of securitisation is invisible to borrowers, who do not even know that their mortgage forms part of a securitised pool. Terms and conditions will remain the same and borrowers will usually continue to deal with the same organisation which initially granted the loan.

Securitisation, therefore, enabled Northern Rock to expand its lending book. Periodically, it would sell on its mortgages by securitisation which, in turn, released further funds with which to lend.

In order to bridge the timing gap between these programmed securitisations it would borrow money short-term from other banks in, what are called, the wholesale money markets. Northern Rock had done this for several years and the process had worked fine.

When a bank borrows in the money markets they pay an interest rate called LIBOR (London Inter-bank Offered Rate), which is usually a little above the Bank of England's base rate. For example, on 2nd January 2007, 3-month LIBOR (the interest rate for borrowing money for 3 months) was 5.32%, while the base rate was 5.00%. The variation of LIBOR over the base rate would affect Northern Rock's profitability.

However, in 2006 this process was working fine, and other mortgage lenders were adopting the same principle too, if not to the same extent.

This funding model (known as "originate to distribute") meant that Northern Rock sold off half of its loans to investors rather than holding them for the full term.

And this was, effectively, Northern Rock's business model.

Its strategy was to fund approximately 25% of its funds from retail deposits (savers), 25% in the wholesale money markets and 50% from securitisation. In 2005, this funding platform – as it is called – was operating swimmingly for Northern Rock, and it was this platform that had enabled it to achieve annual growth of 20%.

Although conceived as early as 1999, this business model was being fully embraced by the board at the time and in particular the Chief Executive, Adam Applegarth. It seemed to be a winning strategy that had delivered year on year.

2006 – A Year of Optimism and Growth

Early in 2006, as I started my first full year in the commercial finance division, how our loans were funded was just about the last thing on my mind. My priority was to go out and get some business.

In contrast to the rest of the business, commercial finance in 2005, where lending growth had been slightly down on 2004, had not had a great year – and that was across the UK. I think that resourcing problems in Leeds and some other offices were the main factor behind that. Well resourced offices such as Manchester and Newcastle had had record years.

Leeds' targets for 2006 reflected the fact that the market had become increasingly competitive. Nevertheless, although targets were reduced to reflect this, I still had to achieve £80 million in new lending in 2006 from a pretty desperate position.

However, we were assured that the board of Northern Rock really valued the commercial business and were very keen to grow it. The offices now were almost fully resourced and improvements had been made to salary and bonus packages to help keep staff on board. This was looking to be more positive news.

During the back end of 2005 and early in 2006, I was starting to get to know better a good proportion of our customers. These were many and varied, they ranged from buy to let landlords to larger property companies. Northern Rock was particularly active in the student property market.

One such investor specialised in buying large student blocks located in key university cities in the North. The guy had been in property for 30 years and had a substantial net worth of over £30 million built up over many years. He felt that Northern Rock had not been particularly enthusiastic towards doing business with him and was on the verge of going to a competitor. I told him that if we weren't keen to lend money to him we might as well close our doors. We subsequently managed to secure a £4 million deal to fund two large student blocks in a major East Midlands based university city.

Another customer, a very experienced commercial property investor in Sheffield who owned a number of multi-let office buildings, was about to move to a competitor bank when I managed to meet him and explain that Northern Rock was keen to help him grow his portfolio further. Again, we were able to build on this relationship over the next two years.

I had a plan to firstly maximise the potential from the customers we had and to secure those relationships, whilst also contacting our orphans, as I called them, those who had somehow lost the relationship they once had with Northern Rock. Fortunately, things worked out well and within six months the Leeds office had lent £53 million against a target for the year of £80 million.

At the same time I had managed to get a new team in place finally, recruiting a new lending manager, Graham, from Barclays, where we had previously worked together. I felt that he had tremendous potential and whilst he was hard-working and sound technically, his real strengths lay in his personable manner and his ability to develop sound business relationships quickly.

Graham was particularly good at getting new business introductions from the broker market. Brokers are intermediaries who help borrowers arrange mortgages (both commercial and residential) in order to find the most competitive deal in the market. Since, by and large, Northern Rock was one of the most competitive lenders, there was huge scope for us to develop the intermediary market and we started to get a fairly high number of new customers.

By now I had recruited an additional support manager and having now got a full team in place, they were getting busy with helping us get the new business onto the books.

Suddenly there was a buzz around the place again.

A good year

The year flew by and an extremely successful one it was. As an office we obtained over 50 new customers that year and achieved a new gross lending figure of £87 million, putting the office in 2nd place in the UK.

A number of factors contributed towards this success. First of all we had good team. We all got on well and had a clear understanding of what was required. We were very customer focused and recognised that the service we gave and the speed with which we responded were key to our success as a unit. We promoted Northern Rock as an organisation very strongly, and raised the awareness in the market of the many strengths it had.

We also had good support from our immediate management who could see the progress being made. And we had good relationships with other parts of the organisation, such as the underwriting and case management teams. Everything seemed to be going well.

Another success locally was the improved working relationship we developed with the local buy to let team who dealt with landlords with small portfolios but who were able to make some extremely good introductions to us.

The year ended with a tremendous sense of achievement and with the feeling that we could, and would, go on to achieve bigger and better things.

On the residential side of the business the success story continued, with gross lending increasing by £23 billion in 2006 to a new high – taking Northern Rock into a position of the 5th largest mortgage lender in the UK. Assets increased by 24% to over £100 billion for the first time and profit growth increased by 19%.

Its market share of new mortgages rose from 7% in 2005, to 13% in 2006 – almost doubling in one year.

And £31 million went to the Northern Rock Foundation, which was Northern Rock's charitable arm, as a donation.

All of Northern Rock's businesses that year did well, and the company announced in August 2006 that all staff would receive a £1,000 pay increase, effective from September. A gesture that I had never experienced before at a bank and which was designed to make all staff feel part of the company's success.

The *Daily Telegraph* Questor Column, in summarising the 2006 results, rated the shares which were then at £11.36 as a "buy" saying:

> This mortgage bank has stripped out so much cost it is consistently able to compete with the lowest offers on the market. As a result, it wins more than its fair share of new business, which drives volumes. And the more business it writes, the better its cost efficiency. The bank plans to leapfrog both Abbey and Lloyds within the next 5 years to become the country's third largest mortgage provider. It is not an unreasonable ambition. Analysts reckon its cost income ratio may be 28.4% within two years and it may have achieved third place by 2010.

This performance was indeed remarkable. I recall reading that this was the 23rd consecutive year that Northern Rock had posted record profits, which was an incredibly impressive achievement. Even the arrears position across the mortgage book was said to be 50% of the industry average. Arrears across the commercial book were almost unheard of. As staff we felt as if we were all part of a major success story and that nothing could stop Northern Rock's continued rise. At that time it was an extremely positive place to work.

Top 3 target

The internal publication of the 2006 results to Northern Rock staff (entitled "Full Time" – alluding to its link with Newcastle United FC) was headed up "Top 3 target".

In his summary of the results, Adam Applegarth said:

> *We are currently a top 5 lender but as we move from being a good to a great company, our goal is to become a "top 3" mortgage lender in the coming years. Let's go for it!*

The future for the business could hardly have been brighter.

Record results, record growth, the lowest cost income ratio of any bank in Europe, the highest mortgage retention rate of any UK lender, and an increasingly valuable brand helped by the high-profile sponsorship of Newcastle United. Northern Rock had become a major institution and the largest single employer in the north-east.

The bank was also increasing its market share dramatically in the first-time buyer market through its "Together" product. This was a packaged mortgage and unsecured personal loan product which gave applicants access to effectively 125% LTV (Loan to Value) against their property – in other words, 125% of the value of the property being mortgaged. However, this was split between the secured element of the property, which was only 95%, and the unsecured element, that made up the remainder. This was considered a market leading product by intermediaries who continued to refer first-time buyers to Northern Rock in droves.

Whilst the product appeared generous, applicants were rigorously credit-scored and staff genuinely considered it to be a low-risk product.

Similarly, on the commercial finance side, there was a "go for growth" message. The 2007 target across the business for new commercial lending was increased by over 50% on that of 2006.

We were promised that we would have all the tools to do the job: more understanding underwriters, keener rates on the bigger deals, a willingness from the top to support growth in commercial lending. We were well up for it!

On the residential side, business continued to boom. 20% of all mortgages being written in the UK were being written by Northern Rock.

Nothing could stop us

2007 started on a wave of optimism. The business had performed well in 2006 across the board. Although interest rates had started to rise, increasing to 5.25% in January 2007, the property market was still performing strongly.

It seemed that absolutely nothing could happen to stop this fantastic progress.

The First Signs of Trouble

There was absolutely no reason to think that the Northern Rock success story would not continue throughout 2007.

Growth expectations within the organisation were high. Within the Leeds Commercial Office our gross lending target was increased to £116 million, which was an increase of over 40% based on our target for 2006. We understood that similar growth expectations were in place across the whole business.

But the market was becoming more difficult.

Interest rates had risen twice in the second half of 2006 – to 4.75% on 4th August and then to 5.00% on 10th November. Then on 12th January they were eased up again to 5.25%. Whilst these rises were not considered to be significant at the time, it was a sign that the government was trying to tackle what was considered to be an overheating of the economy, which carried a real threat of further inflation.

In addition the property market seemed to be tightening. Certainly, good commercial property deals were very hard to come by. Some retail properties were selling at auction for returns of 4.5% and less, at which level the income was struggling to meet interest costs. In other words, investors had to buy property at prices where the rental income was giving them broadly the same return as if they simply put the money on deposit with a bank. As a result, investors who were normally very active in the property market simply sat out.

Nevertheless, there were two factors that were presented to us as being instrumental in helping us achieve these higher targets. The first was a willingness to compete more aggressively on price to obtain the higher quality and higher value deals. The second was a willingness on the part of the underwriting team to adopt a more helpful approach in dealing with commercial finance applications. By this I do not mean that the aim was to relax their risk standards, but rather to communicate more effectively, taking a "yes, if" rather than a "no, because" approach.

This strategy was launched to all Commercial Finance lending-related staff in February at an internal conference which took place at Gosforth Head Office. Whilst many of us were concerned about our ability to achieve this level of growth in a difficult market, at least there was some evidence that Commercial Finance was trying to get its act together and it had ambitions to replicate the success achieved through the sale of residential mortgages.

Also, the various offices, including Leeds, had once again got full strength teams so we all started the year in good spirits.

However, the first real sign of trouble came from an unexpected source.

The bombshell

On Monday 12th March 2007, my Area Director arrived on our doorstep to say that at 11.00am that day an announcement was being made simultaneously to all staff employed in Northern Rock Commercial Finance. This had to be done on a face-to-face basis with the message delivered by a director.

We then had to wait for an hour or so before the news could be delivered to us. It was obvious that this was going to be a serious message and we all sensed, in our office, that whatever this was our jobs clearly might be at risk. Certainly our Area Director did not appear to be relishing delivering the news and looked extremely pale and nervous.

At the appointed time she gathered us together and read a pre-prepared, carefully scripted message which basically advised us that a strategic decision had been made to sell Northern Rock's commercial loan book, which was estimated to stand at around £1.6 billion, in order to free up capital to enable Northern Rock to concentrate on its core business, which was providing residential and buy to let mortgages. We were told that potential interested purchasers would be notified of this and a bidding process would begin. We were advised that Northern Rock would cease to source new commercial mortgage business in its own right. This message came totally out of the blue and was a complete bombshell to us.

It was explained to us that the decision had been brought about by the introduction of the Basel II Accord recommendations – which came into effect from 1st January 2007. The purpose of these recommendations was to create an international standard that banking regulators can use when deciding how much capital banks need to put aside to guard against the types of financial and operation risks banks face. In simple terms, Basel II set out more stringent requirements for capital adequacy in banks than were previously in place.

Basel II was something we knew very little about.

Basel II explained

In the late 1980s, an international regime was put together to ensure that a level playing field operated and that banks had adequate capital to protect the interests of depositors. The Bank for International Settlements, based in Basel in Switzerland, was the body charged with setting up an appropriate framework.

In simple terms, each asset on the balance sheet of a bank was given a weighting of between 0% and 100% (the weighting reflecting the risk of the asset). Corporate debt and unsecured loans were rated as the riskiest assets and carried 100% weighting. Loans secured against residential property were considered to be less risky and were given a 50% risk weighting.

Briefly, each pound lent on a commercial loan had to be supported by a pound's worth of capital. Residential loans required 50% less capital to support them.

A problem with this system was that it was unable to differentiate between the quality of assets. For instance, it was obvious that a loan to Marks and Spencer, for instance, was less of a risk than one to a struggling small business. So, to reflect that, and to give banks more flexibility in situations where risk levels were low, Basel II was introduced.

It is worth mentioning that whilst Basel I offered a single approach to calculating regulatory capital for credit risk, Basel II offered lenders a choice of three approaches. The internal ratings based approach (IRB) was Northern Rock's preferred choice and this allowed it to use Northern Rock's own risk model for this purpose. This model would need to be approved by the Financial Services Authority (FSA).

Northern Rock had no such system in place to estimate the true capital weighting against its commercial loan book, but its residential mortgage risk model, if approved, allowed its risk weighting to reduce from 50% to 15%. So, every £100 lent on residential mortgages would only need £15 of risk-weighted capital to support it, instead of £50.

In anticipation of this being agreed, a decision was made to sell its commercial loan book which would have the beneficial impact of reducing the level of capital required on Northern Rock's balance sheet. The policy was now to focus on its core business, residential mortgages, and the new Basel II regulations appeared to provide a springboard for continued expansion. Agreement from the FSA was eagerly awaited in the shape of its Basel II IRB waiver.

Worrying news

Naturally, this was hugely disappointing and worrying news for us, particularly coming so soon after a very upbeat conference which had the headline message that Northern Rock really wanted to grow its commercial loan book. I wondered, and indeed still wonder, what events had led to such a sudden change in strategy.

Did the board know as far back as February 2007 that the company's capital reserves were under severe pressure?

This news had come out of the blue and we were all shocked by it. It was not clear at that stage whether a buyer would be found for the loan book. And it was certainly not clear what would happen to the staff involved in the commercial finance business, or indeed the office network.

For a few weeks there was great uncertainty around and most people involved in Commercial Finance feared the worst.

At that time one of my support staff had left to go travelling abroad and so, having just appointed a replacement, I was particularly concerned about the newly appointed member of my support staff who had made the move to Commercial Finance from the residential side just the week before. It struck me as rather like joining the Titanic as a crew hand on its maiden voyage.

Jobs secured

However, a few weeks after the original announcement we were told that, whilst the commercial loan book was to be sold, Northern Rock was to continue sourcing commercial loans but effectively as agents for the buyer.

All of our jobs would be safe and business would operate as normal through the current office network. Also, the Head Office functions based at Doxford Park, Sunderland would continue as normal. The intention was for any new business to be sourced via a "forward flow" agreement, whereby any new loans would be ultimately sold to the buyer in return for a commission payment. This was the arrangement used by Northern Rock for its sub-prime residential mortgage business whereby it offered sub-prime loans but then sold them onto Lehmans for a commission payment.

Whilst, in theory, this type of arrangement could work with commercial business, I, and others, had serious doubts about it. Unlike sub-prime mortgage applicants, who are generally low quality borrowers seeking finance from whichever source they can get it, Northern Rock's commercial borrowers were high quality, prime, high value borrowers seeking a long-term relationship with their lender. Furthermore, in terms of market reputation, Northern Rock, in my view, would no longer be seen as being fully committed to the commercial lending market because effectively another bank, and a US based one at that, would be calling the shots.

The three months that followed was a difficult time because we were told that the fact that Northern Rock was seeking bidders for its commercial business could not be disclosed to our commercial borrowers. At the same time we did not want to go out actively promoting commercial business until it was clear who was buying the book and how the forward flow agreement would work.

In the meantime, we still continued to do a substantial amount of business, particularly on the buy to let side. But offices started to see one or two people start to leave to join other banks. This was more a trickle than a flood but a sign that, once again, there was a lot of uncertainty about.

In terms of the impact on Northern Rock's business this was nothing compared with events that were happening outside of the business.

The market continues to deteriorate

The co ntinued rise in interest rates was starting to have an increasing impact on Northern Rock's funding costs.

As mentioned previously, Northern Rock had to borrow 25% of its funds from the money markets to then lend on to its mortgage customers. Typically, these funds were borrowed from other banks on a short-term basis (one to three months) with interest paid at the inter-bank rate LIBOR (London Inter-bank Offered Rate).

Borrowing money from the money markets had never been a problem before. But the problem which arose was that whilst, ordinarily, LIBOR and base rates tracked each other pretty closely, in the early part of 2007 – following three consecutive interest rate rises – LIBOR increased significantly over the base rate.

The problem Northern Rock faced was the mismatch in its lending and borrowing rates. Its lending (mortgage loans) were typically linked to the Bank of England base rate, but its borrowing (from the money markets) was linked to LIBOR. And the cost of the latter was going up faster than the base rate.

Whilst much of our commercial lending was linked to LIBOR, the greater bulk of Northern Rock's residential lending, including the buy to let loans, was not. We therefore soon became aware that this was an area of concern.

(A chart comparing the trend in the base rate and LIBOR can be seen in the Appendix to this book.)

It was this gap between base rate and LIBOR that led Adam Applegarth to issue a profit warning to the London Stock Exchange on 27th June 2007.

The 27th June 2007 statement to the Stock Exchange

The announcement was entitled "Pre-close period statement and Basel II strategic update". It said that in anticipation of receiving our IRB waiver under Basel II, Northern Rock was taking the opportunity to update the market on the resulting evolution of strategy, on current trading performance and the outlook for profits given the current interest rate environment.

As regards strategy it stated that Northern Rock would seek to reduce the proportion of less capital efficient assets held on its balance sheet. This involves maintaining its distribution and manufacturing capability, however higher risk weighted loans would be passed on directly to third parties (e.g. the arrangement with Lehman Brothers for lower quality residential mortgages).

It further said that on 22nd June 2007, Northern Rock completed the sale of approximately £838 million of its commercial secured loans to Lehman Commercial Mortgage Conduit Limited, and conditionally sold a further £732 million of such loans, to be completed in the second half of 2007. In conjunction with the transaction the bank was proposing to negotiate an agreement for future secured Northern Rock originated commercial mortgage loans to be sold on to Lehmans.

The statement went on to discuss the market outlook, lending, costs and income/profit.

On market outlook the statement was broadly positive, with gross lending at the end of May up 13% against the equivalent period of 2006. Whilst rising interest rates were slowing volumes of house moving transactions, lending targets were expected to be achieved.

On lending, gross market share was running at 10% with net market share of residential mortgage lending increasing to 19% because of a robust retention strategy. Arrears levels had increased on 2006 because of higher interest rates, but were in line with expectations.

Costs were continuing to be well controlled.

The key part was in the statement on income and profits.

Basically, since the last trading statement on the 2nd April, there had been two further interest rate rises. Because funds were sourced via Northern Rock's funding platform based on LIBOR and then generally lent on at the Bank of England base rate there was an increasing mismatch between the two and this had impacted on net interest income. The impact of that on net interest income was expected to be around £180 million – £200 million gross. There were some gains to offset this sum and it was anticipated that the pricing mismatch would be corrected when the mortgage deals expired and could be repriced. Nevertheless, the previously anticipated 17% growth in profits was likely to drop to about 15%.

The markets react to the profit warning

I could not believe the reaction of the markets to this trading statement. The share price immediately dropped £1.20 (to £8.50) wiping 12% off Northern Rock's value. This seemed, at the time, a complete overreaction to what was considered to be a short-term funding mismatch.

I suppose at this stage the combination of the sudden sale of its commercial loan book, a profit warning and a 30% fall in Northern Rock's share price from its all-time high point in February 2007, should have been ringing warning bells, even to the most loyal members of its staff.

The market certainly cast its vote with the majority of financial observers now rating Northern Rock as a "sell".

However, the view of the staff – and indeed our customers – at the time was that the negativity against Northern Rock had been greatly overdone. A profit growth of 15% still seemed an impressive figure in what was becoming a difficult market. With Northern Rock's astounding track record of growth the feeling amongst the staff was that the analysts were completely wrong and had simply got it in for the company, perhaps because of jealousy arising from its previous success.

Early rumblings of the sub-prime crisis

What was really driving market sentiment down were concerns over the impact of the American sub-prime crisis on Northern Rock. This crisis had first become news in the earlier part of the year, when it became clear that many American banks had high levels of exposure to sub-prime mortgages – these were lower quality loans lent to people who had a high credit risk or who could not prove their ability to repay.

There had been a major boom in the selling of these loans in the years previously and many people were sold mortgages that they simply could not afford. Property prices had increased as a result of a house market boom driven by the availability of cheap mortgages, but as interest rates in the US increased the trend reversed, borrowers found it increasingly difficult to meet their payments and repossessions soared. This had the effect of bursting the bubble that the availability of sub-prime mortgages had created and the US property market crashed with prices falling by up to 30%. That left banks in a situation where, in many cases, they could not recover their loans because there was a shortfall between what they had lent and the value of the properties securing these loans. The result was that many US banks, and banks around the world, had billions of dollars worth of bad debts.

Northern Rock, it appeared, was not directly involved in these sub-prime loans. Not only was the UK housing market stable, but also the company had no sub-prime loans on its balance sheet. This led me, and many others, to believe that any lack of confidence in Northern Rock would soon pass – the crisis would blow over, the share price would recover and we could all get back to normal.

This sense of complacency was present in an interview with Adam Applegarth for the *Daily Mail* on 27th June, given just five hours after the Stock Exchange announcement was released. In it he said:

> *There are always good days or bad days. The bitterness of the profit warning was sweetened by Northern Rock finally*

receiving its Basle II waiver yesterday which will pave the way for a huge increase in dividends and share buy backs.

We've been waiting three years for this waiver and it comes on the same day as a profit warning. The strange thing is I know the share price has had a good shoeing but I also know the stuff we are announcing today will leave the company in a much better place than it is now in three years' time.

The Basle II waiver meant that only 15% of capital had to be retained to support each residential mortgage, which freed up more capital – although not enough in the event.

With great acuity – that even he may not have quite appreciated at the time – Applegarth remarked at the end of the interview:

There is a finite life in being a Chief Executive. It is rather like being a football manager. Very few people get to choose the time of their leaving.

Meanwhile, life was carrying on very much as normal. The share price continued to fall but nobody seemed that bothered. Indeed, the weakness in the share price was seen as a glorious buying opportunity. After all, how could a fantastically successful company like Northern Rock lose 35% of its value in six months on the back of a 2% adjustment in its profits forecast?

The American sub-prime crisis continued to feature on the news, but this wasn't something that occupied our minds on a day-to-day basis.

However, what the sub-prime crisis had done was to create a shock to the global financial system, and it was this that was concerning the financial analysts. If there was a problem in the financial markets Northern Rock was particularly exposed because it had to source 75% of its funding externally in the money markets.

Although we didn't know it at the time, the fuse had been lit...

A Short Period of Calm

Looking back, the fact that we, as employees, were blissfully unaware of the dangers the sub-prime situation could cause our business, suggests to me that the same was felt by the top brass at Northern Rock, who were clearly of the opinion that the company was well insulated against the potential risks being run.

Concerns over shortages of capital continued to be shrugged off by the company. The interim results internal trading statement issued to staff in July 2007 was extremely upbeat:

> *Not unexpectedly, many of the external commentators who analyse our performance ignore the positives and take a narrow, negative view. As a result our share price has fallen recently. Despite the headwind and all the criticism levelled at us we have announced expected growth in underlying profits in 2007 of around 15%. An excellent performance by any standards! But we do not manage the business for the short term, we look 2-3 years out. This is why we deliberately continued volume lending. Even though we are squeezed in the short term, our excellence in customer service and retention means we can look forward to keeping customers for many years, re-pricing their loans more than once. We have had to take some pain now, but these loans will be good for medium term earnings. Good planning in our view.*

There was no message relating to consolidation or restricting growth – quite the opposite. The whole strategy surrounding selling the commercial loan book and obtaining the Basel II waiver was to free up capital to fund further mortgage expansion and increasing shareholder dividends.

As far as the commercial side of the business was concerned, the emphasis was being placed on improving our buy to let portfolio product to give Northern Rock an edge in the market. We continued to do commercial lending and, in the early days, the relationship with Lehmans (who had bought Northern Rock's commercial loan book) appeared to be working well, but the market had changed. Few commercial property investors were able to find value in the market any more, prices were on the turn and fewer deals were being done.

To assist with this expansion into the buy to let portfolio market we received details of a new buy to let product called a "discounted tracker" to be launched in August. It started, for the lower loan-to-value loans, at an interest rate of just 0.4% above base rate, increasing to 0.9% above base rate after two years. This was an extremely competitive product and, whilst the price varied depending upon the percentage lent in relation to the value of the portfolio, it was still highly competitive, with a top rate of 0.6% reverting to 1.1% over base rate for the more highly leveraged loans.

In conjunction with this new buy to let product being launched we were told that very shortly plans would be announced involving the restructure of Commercial Finance, which was intended to enhance our ability to increase the amount of new lending business.

The fact that this product had been launched and the fact that we were being given very positive messages about both the product and the desire of the business to grow its loan book led us to dismiss from our minds newspaper articles that were predicting some sort of major crisis for Northern Rock.

One such article, which appeared in the *Daily Telegraph* on 15th August asked:

Just how much trouble is Northern Rock in?

A glance at the mortgage lender's share price, which fell 12pc after a profits warning in June and a further 13pc since, would suggest the answer is a heck of a lot.

Northern Rock is being hammered by a liquidity crisis in the wholesale credit markets, where the bulk of its funds for mortgage lending is raised. The markets have virtually shut and, without those funds, it does not have a business. In the most extreme scenario, one analyst said, "Northern Rock would have to stop new lending".

Such an outcome is highly unlikely, but the fact that the thought weighs on investors' minds underlines the bank's precarious state. Lack of liquidity is a structural issue for the mortgage market, but Northern Rock's business model leaves it more exposed than the rest.

More than three quarters of its funding comes from the wholesale markets – by borrowing at the three-month London inter bank offered rate (LIBOR) or by securitising existing mortgages and selling them on to investors. The squeeze on liquidity has made LIBOR unaffordable and killed off demand for "residential mortgage backed securities". Within the past few days, West Bromwich Building Society pulled a planned securitisation because no one wanted the paper.

Northern Rock can still raise wholesale funds at LIBOR but, at the moment, doing so is uneconomical. LIBOR has jumped to 6.37pc but lenders are selling into a mortgage market that prices off the Bank of England's 5.75pc base rate.

In other words, after costs, Northern Rock will have to lend at about 6.75pc to turn the smallest of profits. Rivals, who use cheaper sources of finance than the wholesale markets for half their borrowing, will simply be able to undercut it.

It is this no-win scenario that has prompted Credit Suisse to suggest the bank will miss its revised profit growth target of 15pc this year.

Northern Rock has little control of its destiny now. The liquidity squeeze has been caused by fears about investment banks' exposure to bad debt in the US sub-prime mortgage market and an oversupply of aggressively priced leveraged finance bonds. Until this "indigestion", as commentators describe it, works its way through the system, the liquidity crunch will eat into Northern Rock's prospects. The longer it takes, the worse the damage to Northern Rock

It has a little wriggle room. In early July, before the crisis took hold, it raised more funds than needed and, having outperformed its volume targets in the first half of the year, it can slow down lending and still make its numbers.

A spokesman for Northern Rock said: "Northern Rock has a strong, diversified global funding franchise, raising a balanced mix of funds from both wholesale and retail markets."

Again, strong confirmation that no serious problem existed.

As an employee I genuinely did not think that in August, 2007 Northern Rock had a major problem. Its share price had been hammered, but this was seemingly on the back of a base rate v LIBOR mismatch – which had had a modest impact on profitability. The sale of its commercial book to Lehmans would have realised £1.6 billion or thereabouts in new capital. The successful achievement of the Basel II waiver had reduced pressure on its balance sheet and a new product had been launched at attractive rates designed to capture new buy to let business.

There was clearly a disconnect between the newspaper reports we were seeing daily and what we understood the position to be from within the business. We put this down to creative journalism and general media scaremongering.

On 7th September I flew to San Francisco for a holiday. At this time my office was awaiting details of the proposed restructure and I was happy in the knowledge that all appeared well and that we were putting on significant levels of new business on the back of the new keenly priced buy to let mortgage product.

I asked my colleague, Graham, to e-mail me the details of the restructure which was going to be announced during the first week of my absence.

Little did I know what was really going on behind the scenes.

Behind the Scenes

In August and early September 2007, when, to the outside world, Northern Rock appeared to be functioning normally, its true position was only known, at that time, to a few. What was happening behind the scenes was a rather different picture than the serene "business as usual" stance that the public and we, as members of staff, saw.

On 9th August 2007 the inter-bank market completely froze. In other words, banks stopped lending to each other. The event that triggered this was the announcement by a major French bank, BNP Paribas, that it was suspending three of its asset-backed security funds, saying it could no longer value them accurately because of problems in the US sub-prime mortgage market.

This announcement sent shock waves through an already sensitive money market and it became evident to the board at Northern Rock that it would face severe problems if the markets were to stay frozen for long. The problems were especially severe for Northern Rock because its funding model required mortgage-backed securities and plain mortgages to be securitised, and its next securitisation was scheduled for September 2007.

The Tripartite Standing Committee considers Northern Rock

The Chairman and Chief Executive of Northern Rock first discussed these problems with each other on Friday 10th August.

On the same day, the Financial Services Authority (FSA) contacted the financial businesses that it perceived might be at risk from the freezing of the money markets and Northern Rock was one of those contacted. It replied to the FSA on the next working day, Monday 13th August, alerting the FSA to the potential difficulties that Northern Rock would face if the market freeze continued. Thereafter, the FSA and Northern Rock were in twice daily telephone contact.

On Tuesday 14th August, the first discussions on Northern Rock took place between the Tripartite authorities at deputy level – Mr Sants, Sir John Gieve and a senior Treasury official. The Tripartite Standing Committee includes the Treasury, the Bank of England and the FSA; the system was introduced by Gordon Brown in 1997 to consider matters of financial stability.

On the same day, Tuesday, the Governor of the Bank of England was alerted.

On the following day, Wednesday 15th August, a more detailed conversation took place between the FSA and the Treasury. The Chancellor of the Exchequer was informed about Northern Rock on that day.

On Thursday 16th August, the Chairman of Northern Rock, Dr Matt Ridley, spoke directly to the Governor of the Bank of England by telephone, when the possibility of a support operation was discussed.

On Wednesday 29th August, Sir Callum McCarthy wrote formally to the Chancellor of the Exchequer, Alistair Darling, indicating that the FSA believed that Northern Rock was "running into quite substantial problems".

On Monday 3rd September, the Tripartite Committee met at the level of principals – the Chancellor of the Exchequer, the Chairman of the FSA and the Governor of the Bank of England.

Northern Rock's three options

During this period Northern Rock and the Tripartite authorities had essentially been pursuing a threefold strategy to extricate Northern Rock from its difficulties. The three options pursued were:

1. Northern Rock resolves its liquidity problems through its own actions in short-term money markets and by securitising its debt.

2. Northern Rock obtains the "safe haven" of a takeover by a major retail bank.

3. Northern Rock receives a support facility from the Bank of England guaranteed by the government.

There was considerable overlap between consideration of the three options.

The prospects for a market solution through the money markets, including by securitisation, were pursued until 10th September without success.

The search for a private "safe haven", which would preclude the need for a Bank of England liquidity support operation, was started on 16th August and continued until 10th September.

The possibility of a Bank of England support operation was raised as early as 16th August.

Moral hazard

In August 2007, the Bank of England was approached by banks arguing that the Bank of England should provide additional liquidity, at no penal rate. This request was refused, the main reason being the risk of "moral hazard". In essence, the argument is that should the central bank act – and effectively provide extra liquidity at different maturities against weaker collateral – markets would, especially if the liquidity was provided at little or no penalty, take it as a signal that the central bank would always rescue them should they take excessive risk and get into difficulties. Such a signal would lead to ever more risk taking, and the next crisis would consequently be greater than it otherwise would have been.

This may not have necessarily been a view that was shared by the FSA, but nevertheless it was a view that subsequently prevailed. However, it is worth noting that the Bank of England, the European Central Bank and the Federal Reserve each pursued a different course of action in response to the money market turmoil. Only the Bank of England took no contingency measures at all during August.

The European Central Bank appeared to attach far less weight to the moral hazard argument than the Bank of England. Instead, it adopted a pro-active approach in resolving what it saw as a practical problem of a faltering market resulting from banks losing confidence in each other. Although the ECB injected no net additional liquidity in August, it did alter the timing and term profile of its regular operations, front loading its credit supply towards the start of August, and in doing so it appeared to satisfy the immediate liquidity requirements of the Eurozone banking sector.

The safe haven option

With regard to the second option – the "safe haven" option – Northern Rock began to pursue this on 16th August, acting behind the scenes and with its advisors to encourage an offer for the company to be made. Two institutions showed an interest in acquiring Northern Rock. One came to nothing but the other, believed to be Lloyds TSB, showed a very specific interest.

Whilst it is not clear how far these discussions went, it was clear that any takeover would be conditional on the Bank of England providing a backstop facility for a certain period of time to cover the liquidity issues that Northern Rock had. The facility required was reported to be as much as £30 billion for a two-year period at market rates.

Again, this was a potential solution that Mervyn King was not prepared to agree to. He did not see it as the function of a central bank to facilitate the takeover of one bank by another through the provision of loans or guarantees – let alone to the tune of £30 billion!

Only one option remained

So on Monday 10th September, Northern Rock abandoned its attempts at securitisation and its pursuit of a safe haven and was left with one remaining option – a support facility from the Bank of England. Northern Rock envisaged the operation as a backstop facility that would only be drawn down should the other possible funding avenues prove inaccessible.

At the 3rd September meeting, referred to earlier, it appears that a decision in principle to provide Northern Rock with support was taken. The preference, when it became clear on the 10th September that this was the only remaining option available, was for a covert operation. However, this idea was abandoned on Tuesday 11th September for two reasons. Firstly, there was a requirement upon the board of Northern Rock to make an announcement to the Stock Exchange about the situation. Secondly, there were potentially practical difficulties involved in a covert operation should details of this leak.

Also, it was felt by Mervyn King that if the Bank of England provided support to Northern Rock on an undisclosed basis it might be in breach of the Market Abuse Directive, which is a piece of European legislation, and whilst the rules on this were not clear this was a consideration at the time.

In any event Northern Rock itself came to the conclusion that it was best to make a public statement that it had the facility. The board believed that the sign of reassurance of having a facility from the Bank of England would help it and that this would shore up public confidence, thereby preventing a run on the bank.

So plans were drawn up to make an appropriate announcement to be released on Monday 17th September.

The Run on the Bank

In the second week of September I was on holiday in America. Whilst there I was expecting an announcement about a restructure of Northern Rock Commercial Finance and had primed my colleague, Graham, to e-mail me with full details.

The details came through on 10th September. On the back of plans to dramatically expand the buy to let portfolio side of the business we were to increase our team headcount by two, appointing a new Commercial Finance Manager and an office-based Assistant Commercial Finance Manager. In addition, the sales roles (i.e. my role and the two Commercial Finance Managers) were to be home-based and fully focused on developing business through intermediaries. The lending target for the Leeds office was to be £25 million for the quarter. The brief was to sell as actively as possible our new competitive portfolio buy to let product with which we had already had a lot of success.

The restructure made sense. I had always thought Northern Rock had operated the commercial side of its business in a way I had not seen since the early 1990s, when bank managers were all office-based and had a whole raft of personal assistants and secretaries supporting their lending activities. That was not how the Business Development Managers in Northern Rock's indirect residential mortgage business operated, and I saw this as a move to bring commercial into the 21st century.

I was therefore starting to contemplate how I would tackle this new role on my return to the UK.

14th September 2007

Then, on 14th September, I received the following e-mail from Graham:

> *Massive blow! Northern Rock has approached the Bank of England for money. We have been bailed out at the 11th hour. I have some major deals on the go and today will destroy all confidence in NR.*

This came totally out of the blue. I couldn't believe it.

It was 7.30am in the morning on 14th September in Monterey, California, eight hours behind UK time where it was 3.30pm in the afternoon. A Google search quickly showed the scenes which are still etched on everyone's minds when thinking about the Northern Rock crisis. There were massive queues outside the branches and what can only be described as panic as people rushed to withdraw their savings.

The news of the bail out had been released in the UK on the evening of Thursday 13th September by BBC Business Editor, Robert Peston. The article was headed up:

> *Northern Rock gets bank bail out*

The article said that the decision by the Bank of England to give emergency financial support to Northern Rock did not mean that the bank was in danger of going bust – but it was clear from the reaction of the UK public that they weren't hanging around to read the small print!

The fact that this news had been leaked to the BBC – before any official announcement was made by the authorities or indeed Northern Rock – completely wrong-footed the FSA, the Bank of England and the Treasury, who all remained silent over the weekend. The Tripartite authorities had its first real crisis to deal with and was found wanting.

A chaotic three days

What followed was a chaotic three days where Northern Rock branches were besieged by customers desperate to withdraw their savings. Staff manfully worked into the evenings to cope with the onslaught, branches opened early and stayed open late to cope with the queues. The online withdrawal facility ceased to function under the strain, leading to accusations that the bank was going bust and was not allowing withdrawals.

Staff were opening branches at 7.30am and keeping them open to 6.30pm in the evening, just to cope with the incessant stream of people drawing out their savings. I heard of some branches that had had people queuing since 5.00am.

Some people were only withdrawing small sums of money. It didn't matter – panic had set in. One guy, who withdrew £300, admitted that he was only there because he wanted to be on the telly. Another, a pensioner, had apparently queued up for three hours to withdraw just £1.87 and close his account.

Even the weather didn't help. One might suppose that if it had been raining that particular weekend many of the savers who had queued up to withdraw small sums might not have bothered. However, the weather was lovely.

By and large though, the vast majority of people in these queues were hard-working ordinary folk who had real concerns about the safety of their savings. In the event nobody, including Northern Rock or the Bank of England, has blamed them for doing what they did. It was natural, given the lack of clarity at the time.

Northern Rock staff at that time experienced a tremendous team spirit as everyone pitched in together to deal with the crisis. Certainly, Commercial Finance staff helped to try to reassure depositors queuing outside local Northern Rock branches and many staff worked extremely long hours during the immediate run.

The whole situation appeared to be ludicrous. The UK which had, until then, achieved a reputation for being one of the world's leading financial centres had degenerated overnight into appearing like a banana republic. The images of queues outside Northern Rock branches snaking several hundred yards along the streets were unprecedented and caused shockwaves both in the UK and around the world.

One of the reasons for the level of panic had been as a result of the rather complex guarantee arrangements that existed for savers. The problem was that out of the £35,000 of deposits guaranteed by the government only the first £2,000 of savings was 100% guaranteed, with the remaining £33,000 only 90% guaranteed. Above that there was no guarantee at all. Whilst initially savers had probably not been aware that some of their savings could potentially be at risk, the media coverage that followed the initial run actually highlighted the situation to the public at large.

And that was the issue. In the absence of a 100% guarantee for all savers there was a risk of loss, and it was that risk that brought Northern Rock savers in droves to withdraw their money.

Trying to make sense of it all

I was sitting in my hotel room watching a news item about O.J. Simpson, who had been busted in a Las Vegas hotel room with two henchman. The next item that appeared was the scene of a queue outside a branch of Northern Rock. I had to remind myself that I was in America. I doubt very much whether the average American citizen had ever heard of Barclays, let alone a mortgage lender like Northern Rock.

But they had certainly heard about it now!

The newsreader warned that the current financial crisis that had claimed this small mortgage lender in the UK could have a similar impact on a US bank "if we are not careful". The irony was not lost on me. A global crisis that had started in the US through excessive sub-prime mortgage lending had claimed the scalp of a UK mortgage lender that had not been engaging in sub-prime lending at all in its own right.

I could not believe what I was seeing. I read as many online UK newspaper articles as I could find. Whilst they highlighted the point that depositors' money should be safe, and that the problem had been brought about by the drying up of the wholesale money markets, there were those quite prepared to place the blame squarely with Northern Rock's management.

Liberal Democrat Treasury spokesman, Vince Cable, was reported in the *Guardian* as saying:

> *This is a very serious development indeed and it was entirely predictable, since Northern Rock is one of those banks which have been aggressively increasing its market share by offering mortgages at multiples of income well in excess of prudent levels. It is not surprising that in the growing credit crunch the market should start to become alarmed about its future viability.*

This view was supported by a number of financial commentators who seized upon Northern Rock's rapid rate of growth as a major factor behind its problems.

I e-mailed to Graham:

> *The press are giving Northern Rock an absolute slating. From a corporate perspective this appears to have been a total mismanagement of the company's affairs coupled with a lack of honesty about its true position. It will take some time, if ever, to restore any faith in the company and it will be very interesting to see how things unfold. Needless to say if NR is faced with a large exit of customers and staff as a result of this debacle it need not be surprised. The share price*

has dropped by over £2! Hoping for better news when I get back!

The next day Graham responded:

Sorry to panic you last night – I had had a few beers and misread the situation. The main issue is not our corporate borrowers, who are quite understanding, it is mainly the pensioners who are withdrawing funds from branches and the media who have added to the problems. If the funds (from the Bank of England) had been allocated without press knowledge there would not be an issue. GMTV also suggested that people should draw out their savings as soon as possible. They didn't say that about Barclays who have also been to the Bank of England for money. Typically, most of the people queuing do not really understand the situation. I would suggest the mismanagement comment is quite harsh as no-one could have predicted the issues we have today.

I was trying to make some sort of sense of all this. All I knew was that for months, as the share price fell, Northern Rock's management had been saying that there was no problem other than a mismatch between LIBOR and the base rate, which had squeezed its profit margins. Whilst analysts had suggested all along that Northern Rock was particularly vulnerable to a potential funding problem because it sourced 75% of its capital from the wholesale markets. And yet the company's management had given the impression to the media that it was funding its mortgage lending activities without any difficulty and that there was nothing to be concerned about.

Now it was facing a situation whereby it had been bailed out by the Bank of England and its position had been splashed across the UK newspapers with photographs of massive queues of people outside branches desperate to withdraw their money, and over the weekend not one announcement was made by either the FSA or the Bank of England, nor indeed the Chancellor to quell the sense of panic.

Back in the UK, Adam Applegarth made a Stock Exchange announcement on the 14th September which had the dual role of covering the current crisis and providing the markets with a further profits warning.

This announcement was necessary in the light of the continuing extreme global liquidity crisis – lack of available cash on a worldwide scale – which has prevailed over a month. In simple terms, banks have almost stopped lending money to each other, and when they do it is at an extremely high cost. In addition, other sources of funding have substantially dried up. Investors have become increasingly and irrationally nervous of investing in things like mortgage backed securities – our Granite securitisation programme is a good example. [Granite was an offshore based company used by Northern Rock to securitise some of its mortgages.]

The start of this, as you may have read in the press or seen on TV, lies in the US and concerns about their sub prime mortgage lending. This has nothing directly to do with Northern Rock, but the ensuing global crisis that has followed is entirely out of our control and we are not immune from it. The situation is affecting all banks, not just us, but because we raise much of our funds in global markets we have been significantly affected at an early stage.

As a result, we have had to slow down lending activities and will continue to do so until markets normalise.

The statement went on to say that the 2007 pre- tax profits were likely to reduce to £500 million from £540 million, which was still a creditable performance in the circumstances.

Adam Applegarth then took the opportunity to take a swipe at the press:

Regrettably, following a period of brutal treatment in the press and broadcast media recently, this announcement is likely to generate further adverse coverage of Northern Rock and a further hit on our share price. This is all very frustrating when we have done nothing wrong. Our current situation is not due to poor administration or mismanagement of the business – we are literally victims of a global financial crisis.

Finally, the statement went on to explain why an additional funding facility with the Bank of England was being sought and referred to the fact that other banks around the world had set up similar facilities with their own central banks.

Back in the States I e-mailed Graham again on Monday 17th September.

The press reports about NR do not make good reading. Shares down again 160p to 2.80 when I last looked. It is rather surreal seeing this all unfold from the other side of the Atlantic. God knows what it is like at the coal face. 9 billion pounds drawn out of deposit accounts over the weekend. One newspaper report says the game is up as regards Northern Rock remaining a stand-alone company. As you say a break up or buy out is the likely outcome. This would be the first banking collapse since the Bank of Credit and Commerce in the 1980s and it is just our luck to be in the middle of it. Despite all the negative things I have said about Barclays, at least they didn't collapse whilst I was on holiday! Alcohol consumption rising at a similar pace to which the share price is falling. We arrive in New York tomorrow.

On Monday 17th September queues were seen outside Northern Rock branches for the third day running. Eventually, later that day, Alistair Darling finally announced that the government was guaranteeing 100% of all savers' deposits in Northern Rock and would provide a similar guarantee to any other bank in a similar situation.

On Tuesday 18th September the queues finally stopped.

The transatlantic e-mails continued to flow. From Graham:

Saved at the eleventh hour by the government. A much rosier picture today as queues have gone and savers are starting to open accounts again. It is the most surreal 4 days I have ever had in a bank. Most deals are still moving forward. The key is now, who will take on the Rock? English banks have been refused by the FSA, so a foreign contingent looks like the most likely option. The BTL product is still available.

I arrived back in the UK on 23rd September. The Northern Rock crisis was, by far, the hottest news in the press. In the two weeks I had been away the share price had fallen 72%, from £6.51 to £1.94.

The Northern Rock brand was now considered to be worthless.

And all this happened while I was away on a short holiday!

Back in the office

So what greeted me when I got back to my job in Northern Rock Commercial Finance in Leeds?

Obviously all the staff had been shocked by the run, but few at that stage blamed the bank's management for what had happened. Most saw it as a combination of events that could not have been foreseen and blamed the run on both the press leak and the lack of incisive action by the government.

Indeed, the view from within Northern Rock was that the company was very much the victim of a global financial crisis totally outside its control, and neither the company nor the regulatory bodies could have possibly foreseen what could be described as a kind of financial Tsunami.

There was also a feeling that the bank's troubles were being actively celebrated by the media. Many staff believed that the authorities handling the crisis (the FSA, the Bank of England and the Treasury) had messed it up. It was noted, with some exasperation, that other banks who had sought similar support in the liquidity crisis (Barclays being reported as one) had emerged unscathed.

At the time there was much speculation in the press that a number of other banks were facing difficulties similar to Northern Rock but had either escaped the attention of the UK press or had managed to borrow funds from the ECB (European Central Bank) on an undisclosed basis, therefore avoiding the glare of publicity that had led to the run on Northern Rock. It appeared to me to be rather unfair that loans given by the ECB to European banks were undisclosed, whilst the Bank of England facility had been openly publicised. Unfortunately for Northern Rock it did not have an established European presence and therefore could not access funding from the ECB that was available to most other UK banks.

"Rock Steady"

It would be fair to say that the reaction to the crisis from some staff was one of denial. They regarded this as a blip and expected everything to return to normal in a matter of weeks. Brokers were still very supportive of the Northern Rock brand and many borrowers I spoke to at the time thought the crisis would blow over. There was something of a bunker mentality within the organisation.

Soon after the run T-shirts were issued to all Northern Rock staff entitled "Rock Steady". I saw these worn by staff in branches; they were designed to create the impression that Northern Rock would continue as normal despite its problems and to also act as a statement of solidarity.

However, confidence is a strange thing. Once lost, it is so hard to recover. And so, although everything looked the same, it wasn't. Underneath all the bravado I think that most people knew it. Already, just a few days after the run, the press was reporting that the brand was effectively dead. Talks of a takeover, or even break up, of the company emerged very quickly.

The proposed recruitment of the additional Commercial Finance Manager for my office was abandoned.

Although the queues stopped, the main activity in the branches was in the shape of more savers continuing to withdraw funds – despite the government guarantee. Despite savers who had withdrawn funds in the run being offered a refund of their penalties if they reopened their accounts there were few takers.

These events were unbelievable but they were just the start of a process that eventually led to the demise of both Northern Rock and potentially the Commercial Finance business within a few months.

Why did the run happen?

Inevitably, the handling of events leading up to the run on Northern Rock came under scrutiny:

How was it allowed to happen?

Why had it taken so long for the government to announce a full depositor's guarantee which effectively stopped the run?

Could the run on Northern Rock have been avoided completely?

Many of the answers to these questions lie in a publication by the House of Commons Treasury Committee entitled "The Run on the Rock", which looks at the background to the run and the way in which the crisis was handled. In addition, much of the background to the behind the scenes events during the period leading up to the run on Northern Rock, was revealed in the Treasury Select Committee Hearing of 16th October 2007, and Mervyn King's Radio Four interview on 6th November 2007.

However, I think it would be helpful to briefly summarise the chain of events here.

It will be recalled that having agreed to provide Northern Rock with an emergency funding facility on or around 11th September

2007, the intention was to formally make an announcement on Monday 17th September in such a way as not to cause panic. The reason for delaying the announcement was to allow time for Northern Rock to increase the bandwidth of its website and to make other arrangements for handling customers and others affected by the announcement.

On the afternoon of Thursday 13th September, rumours in the market started in relation to the proposed operation to support Northern Rock. At 4.00pm on that day, the Tripartite Standing Committee met at deputies level and decided to bring forward the announcement of the operation to 7.00am on Friday 14th September.

The announcement was to be made in the following terms:

> The Chancellor of the Exchequer has today authorised the Bank of England to provide a liquidity support facility to Northern Rock against appropriate collateral and at an interest rate premium. This liquidity facility will be available to help Northern Rock to fund its operations during the current period of turbulence in financial markets while Northern Rock works to secure an orderly resolution to its current liquidity problems ... The FSA judges that Northern Rock is solvent, exceeds its regulatory capital requirement and has a good quality loan book.

Unfortunately, before the provision of emergency liquidity assistance by the Bank of England could be announced formally, the outlines of the operation were reported by the BBC at 8.30pm on Thursday 13th September.

The general view is that the leak was instrumental in precipitating the run on Northern Rock because it created panic amongst its investors and savers. Indeed, no matter what the subsequent formal announcement might say, the damage had been done at that stage.

None of the formal communications made at that time sufficiently reassured investors and savers to the point that the run stopped. There was no communication from the authorities over the fateful weekend. A television appearance by Adam Applegarth, CEO of Northern Rock, aimed at reassuring investors failed to stop further queues forming on the following Monday morning.

Eventually, after the announcement on 17th September of the provision of a 100% government guarantee to all existing depositors, the run stopped.

Why had it taken so long to make the announcement of the 100% guarantee?

In a subsequent interview on BBC Radio Four, Mervyn King explained that whilst a decision had been made earlier to reassure the public by providing a 100% government guarantee to depositors, no formal announcement of this could be made until the government's legal advisors had decided what form of words could be used to deliver this message, and that took time.

In other words, in making such an announcement, there had to be absolute clarity about what exactly was being guaranteed and getting the statement right was crucial.

In the meantime, over that weekend no assurances could be made by the government to depositors because, in theory at that time, a portion of their savings could have been at risk and to announce that savers had no cause for concern would have not been true.

The consequences of the continuance of the run for Northern Rock were immense, and the run on deposits which took place between Friday 14th September and Monday 17th September was the central element in the problems it faced subsequently.

The speed and extent of withdrawals meant that the Bank of England's emergency facility – which had been envisaged as a backstop – actually needed to be called upon almost immediately.

The Immediate Aftermath of the Run

What struck me in the immediate aftermath of the run was the sheer volume and intensity of the media coverage about the Northern Rock crisis. Some of the reporting was less than fair.

At least the media were having fun

One particular story I read was about some of Northern Rock's staff attending a luxury weekend corporate event in a five star hotel in Marbella. The implication was that whilst ordinary people were desperately trying to withdraw their hard-earned savings, some directors and staff were living it up at the company's – and now the taxpayers' – expense.

The event in question did indeed take place. It was called the Director's Club and this was a half-yearly reward scheme for the top performers in the company. It was no different to other performance-related schemes offered by other companies except that partners were invited to it too.

The truth is that the Director's Club event in Marbella was intended to reward staff for their performance in the first half of 2007. The event was organised well in advance of Northern Rock's problems being revealed. But the timing could hardly have been worse. I understand that the senior directors due to attend this weekend chose not to do so in an effort to deal with the problems at home. That did not get reported in the press, of course.

It was not long before Northern Rock acquired various nicknames, such as Northern Wreck or Northern Crock. It did appear to us that the media was rather enjoying having the opportunity of reporting on the demise of this once proud organisation.

I recall having a discussion with my Area Director fairly soon after my return to the office from holiday. She was from Newcastle and was absolutely devastated about what had happened. But what had upset her most was that Ant and Dec had done a sketch on their 'Saturday Night Takeaway' programme aimed at Northern Rock. In the sketch, Dec "quit" the show and demanded a huge pay off, the next clip showed him carrying a cheque towards a branch of Northern Rock before shaking his head and walking away.

She was absolutely livid that Ant and Dec, who were both from the north-east, should use their show to take a cheap shot at Northern Rock. This had apparently upset many people in the north-east. Indeed, the ITV website forums had featured criticism of the joke and it released a statement which said that the sketch was a tongue-in-cheek reflection of the biggest news of the week and was never intended to upset or criticise anyone. However, as one can imagine, sensitivities in the north-east at that time were running high.

Staff try to carry on as normal

I recall that during the first few weeks after the run there was virtually no official internal communication to the staff except for a personal heartfelt note from Adam Applegarth thanking the staff for the enormous contribution they had made during what was an extremely difficult time.

Despite the obvious problems Northern Rock was facing the mood was one of optimism and defiance. Many staff were of the opinion that fears of a crisis in the banking sector were overblown and once things had stabilised Northern Rock would simply carry on its business as normal albeit at a slower pace. There were few at that time who considered that the game was up.

Northern Rock was also getting plenty of backing from the north-east, where many past recipients of charitable donations from the Northern Rock Foundation were pledging their support. Bobby Robson, the ex-Newcastle and England football manager, was reported as planning to open an online account with Northern Rock in the immediate aftermath of the run. He was quoted by BBC News as saying:

> All I can say is that Northern Rock has been very supportive and has shown great allegiance to the sporting fabric of the north-east for many years and I feel it is only right to support them at this moment. It is a very influential and thriving company and a great benefactor to many people in the north-east and that's why I am offering my support!

Unfortunately though, Bobby Robson was in the minority. Our local branch at Briggate in Leeds was reporting that although the run had stopped, the bulk of customers calling into the branch were either withdrawing savings or closing their accounts.

Back in the office, business continued as normal, at least for a while. Whilst some other lenders had withdrawn from the market as a result of the credit crunch, Northern Rock continued to lend at all levels although adjustments were made to the pricing so that they started to become uncompetitive.

The problem was that the cost of funds in the market was simply too great to offer the same deals that were previously on offer. Even the Bank of England support was at a premium interest rate, 1% over base rate, we believed. As a result of this, business started to dry up.

Very soon after the run the company announced a freeze on recruitment, although said it was fiercely protective of existing jobs and would be working closely with the staff union with a view to maintaining the future of its workforce.

The company car scheme was also frozen; where a change in company car was due new vehicles were not being ordered.

Press speculation

Meanwhile, in the press different stories were circulating on a daily basis.

The *Guardian* ran a feature on 17th September where you could vote on whether or not you thought that Northern Rock's brand was finished. I have to say that I never bothered to look up the outcome.

The share price was down at £2.82 that night from a February high of £12.51, and many newspapers were speculating about what the shares in Northern Rock might ultimately be worth in a takeover scenario. An article entitled:

> *Could Northern Rock go for 1p per share?*

appeared in the *Daily Mail* on the 18th September. In it, the newspaper argued that the longer the crisis was to go on without a takeover the lower the share price would get. It was fairly clear from reports at an early stage after the run that there was not a queue of suitors lining up to bid for Northern Rock. Not surprisingly the credit crisis that had ultimately caused Northern Rock to run out of cash was making it equally difficult for another bank to step in and buy it.

Towards the end of the *Daily Mail* article it mentioned that an analyst at broker Panmure Gordon suggested that the takeout price could be somewhere between 1p and 400p, depending upon the quality of the loan book and how long it would take to find a buyer. On that basis the headline rather smacked of creative journalism, but this was not the only article published that dramatised Northern Rock's situation to the fullest extent.

Other articles published at the time preferred to focus on the causes behind the crash and how it was handled. The *Financial Times* reported that the Conservatives attacked the government's "four days of indecision" over the Northern Rock crisis.

This article also reported Dr Matt Ridley, Northern Rock's Chairman as saying:

> *If we can get through this and get to calm financial markets, we do intend to rebuild. If other options become available we will consider them too.*

Meanwhile, the Bank of England injected £4.4 billion into the financial markets to "offset the disturbance of the Northern Rock rescue. Other news was that Northern Rock's largest shareholder, Baillie Gifford, had sold most, if not all, of its 6% holding in Northern Rock, realising a loss of up to £200 million.

Initial takeover hopes fade

Hopes of an expeditious takeover of Northern Rock had faded very quickly. It was reported that at least 12 UK and continental banks had rejected potential takeover moves. These included HSBC, Barclays, Lloyds TSB, Royal Bank of Scotland, Banco Santander and Crédit Agricole. The problem was that the sheer size of Northern Rock's mortgage book, at £100 billion, was considered to be too big to take on, particularly during a credit crunch.

There was pressure from the press for the board at Northern Rock to resign in the aftermath of the run, and the board was also strongly criticised for pressing ahead with the payment of the interim dividend to shareholders scheduled for payment on 26th October at a cost of £59 million. It was argued that the decision to pay the dividend was ill-judged despite Northern Rock's apparent solvency because the Bank of England had already provided £3 billion in support, so the taxpayers were effectively underwriting this transaction. Inevitably, on 25th September, Northern Rock announced that the interim dividend would not be paid.

Adam Applegarth released a statement to the Stock Exchange to this effect and also confirmed that Northern Rock had received a number of approaches from third parties regarding a variety of options for its future. Because a number of potential buyers had been ruled out, there were rumours that these enquiries were from hedge funds looking to acquire the business with a view to breaking it up.

As you can imagine, the press coverage, including the rumours and speculation that went with it, were deeply unsettling for Northern Rock's staff. However, by and large, few people were leaving the company at this stage although, undoubtedly many, including me, were considering their options. Most people I spoke to were strongly of the opinion that Northern Rock could still remain intact as a company and that would be the best solution. It was, however, becoming increasingly clear that Northern Rock's future was looking increasingly unlikely to be in its own hands.

In late September it emerged that two private equity firms had shown an interest in acquiring Northern Rock. One was J.C. Flowers and the other Cerberus.

In the meantime Richard Lambert, CBI Director General, was reported as saying that the near collapse of Northern Rock had revealed deep flaws in Britain's tripartite system of financial regulation:

> The reputation and standing of the UK as a world financial leader has been tarnished. Outside the movies, a run on the bank is something that happens in a banana republic. That one should have happened under our noses, in a mature and prosperous country, such as the UK, is almost unimaginable.

It became clear to me, at a fairly early stage, that this was not just about a run on Northern Rock, but about a much wider political situation in respect of which much more was about to unfold. The press were not only critical of the way Northern Rock had been managed, but also of how the whole matter had been handled by the government. It was starting to have repercussions way beyond those merely relating to the banking sector.

There was also something rather strange about going home every night and seeing some reference to one's employers either on the TV or highlighted in one of the newspapers. Also, working for Northern Rock suddenly became a conversation piece at every corporate event I went to. Every conversation I had with a customer, broker, valuer or solicitor inevitably started with a discussion about Northern Rock, what was happening to it and what I thought might happen next.

The inevitable jokes emerged, such as:

Northern Rock Warning – The Crisis Continues

The knock-on from the Northern Rock crisis and the US sub-prime market in Japan shows no signs of letting up.

In the last seven days Origami Bank has folded, Sumo Financial has gone belly up and Bonsai Bank plans to cutback some of its branches.

Yesterday it was announced that Karaoke Bank is up for sale and will go for a song.

Today, shares in Kamikaze Bank were suspended after they nose-dived and ultimately crashed, while 500 back-office staff at Karate Bank also got the chop.

Analysts also report that there is something fishy going on at Sushi Bank and with redundancies likely staff fear they will get a raw deal.

It certainly was interesting to be in the public eye even if for the wrong reasons.

Into October and business starts to dry up

September came to a close with a resolution to the crisis being no closer. As we moved into October the business was still functioning relatively normally, although lending volumes had reduced. There were also real concerns amongst some commercial borrowers about the potential longevity of the relationship they might have with Northern Rock.

Early in October a number of things happened that started to tell us that things had really changed.

Firstly, on 4th October, Northern Rock axed two thirds of its residential mortgage product range, at the same time scaling back on its enhanced income multiples. Those products remaining were priced at the top end of the spectrum and above the rates offered by the competition. In commercial finance the same thing happened and commercial loan interest margins were increased by 0.75% from where they were previously. The buy to let portfolio margins increased to 1.89% over base rate. In addition, the maximum loan-to-value we could do was eased back from 85% to 80% in September, dropping further in October to 75%.

Other lenders were taking similar actions because of the impact of the credit crunch and the increasing cost of funds. Indeed, some lenders stopped lending to new customers completely.

However, the impact of this was that new lending started to completely dry up.

On the same day, I picked my laptop up from Northern Rock's head office in Gosforth and underwent a one hour training session. The purpose of being home-based was to pro-actively go out and develop business for the company. This was going to prove enormously difficult given the situation Northern Rock was in, the market and the lack of competitiveness of its products.

It was probably at about this point when the realisation set in that this was not going to be a blip and that something very serious was now happening. Potential bidders were now circling the company in the shape of Virgin and Olivant, and it was clear to everyone that a takeover was now the likely outcome for Northern Rock.

The mood was epitomised by a colleague from the local branch who I met briefly before going into a meeting there. His desk was completely clear. The biggest problem he had was keeping the staff busy. There were virtually no mortgage enquiries. Across his room beside the door he had a green frog (Northern Rock's logo) dangling with some string around its neck in the shape of a noose. That said it all really.

Northern Rock Directors Grilled by MPs

House of Commons Treasury Select Committee Hearing – 16th October

On 16th October, I was in the office together with my team and my Area Director. On this day key members of the Northern Rock board had been summoned to appear before the House of Commons Treasury Select Committee for a grilling on their role in the events leading up to the run on the bank.

The four members of the board to be questioned were Dr Matt Ridley (Chairman), Adam Applegarth (Chief Executive), Sir Derek Wanless and Sir Ian Gibson (both Non-Executive Directors).

This was the first occasion since the run on Northern Rock that such a high-profile interview had taken place. I wanted to understand first-hand the events that had led up to the crash so this was compelling viewing – we all watched it avidly.

I propose to highlight the main areas of significance that emerged from it.

The hearing was certainly an eye opener (if a hearing can ever be described as such).

The four about to be questioned looked most uncomfortable, as indeed they had every right to be. They were first asked to introduce themselves to the committee and then Dr Ridley was questioned about the background to his appointment as Chairman, which was in 2004 after thirteen years on the board.

The questioning was very direct, to the point of being, on occasions, aggressive. The bulk of the questions were directed at the Dr Ridley, who, it has to be said, gave a rather nervous, stumbling performance, and Chief Executive, Adam Applegarth, who dealt with the questions rather more assuredly.

I recall both of them being asked about their background qualifications. It emerged that the Chairman had never been involved in any other banking business apart from Northern Rock, and the Chief Executive admitted to not having a banking qualification. Blimey, I've got more banking qualifications than both of them, I thought.

I later discovered that Dr Ridley was a zoologist by profession and had written a number of books on various related subjects. His doctorate was in the mating habits of pheasants.

Business model

Asked if he was at ease with the business model adopted by Northern Rock, Dr Ridley replied that Northern Rock's business model was a good one in that it allowed the achievement of good credit quality in its loan book and steady growth over a number of years. However, the business model proved unable to cope with an unexpected, unpredicted seizure of the money markets in August. He maintained that the board were aware of the risk of tightening in the credit markets throughout, and via Northern Rock's Risk Committee had been continually assessing and stress-testing for different risks. It was expected that Northern Rock's good credit quality and diverse funding platform would stand it in good stead. The concept of all capital markets freezing up for an extended and prolonged period was not considered by either the board or the regulatory authorities. In Dr Ridley's words:

> We were hit by an unexpected and unpredictable concatenation of events.

Risk and credit policy

A number of questions were raised about why the board had taken no action when the FSA had warned in a report in April of a potentially "sharp reduction in liquidity" in the markets; why did expansion continue despite this and other warnings?

Adam Applegarth said that in March, Northern Rock informed the FSA of a change of strategy which related to moving onto a "slower growth model". Whilst the comment seemed to be accepted by the Committee, and the questioning moved on to other areas, the idea of a "slower growth model" was news to us, as a strategy to slow down the rate of growth had certainly not appeared in sales communications. However, the growth slowdown was not substantial – moving from 20%-22% annual growth down to 16%-17%. One committee member commented:

> I suppose I must have been running dull businesses in the past, but certainly a growth rate of 16%, which in real terms is 12% or 13%, would seem pretty aggressive to me.

The main defence here was that all aspects of Northern Rock's risk and credit policy had been regularly stress-tested by the FSA and were considered adequate. What was not stress-tested was the ability of Northern Rock to cope with a sudden and prolonged seizure of the financial markets.

Sir Derek Wanless was also questioned about Northern Rock's aggressive growth strategy. He maintained that it was a growth strategy that had been in place since 2000, when he joined the board. It was not aggressive; it was clearly visible to the market and a diverse series of funding sources were put in place to support it.

Sir Derek was the head of Northern Rock's Risk Committee and had also been in a senior position with National Westminster bank. He was asked about the role of the Risk Committee in the months leading up to the run. He was questioned fairly aggressively about his credentials:

> The BBC were saying in their website that you were seen as having driven NatWest into an ill-advised series of deals, in particular a foray into the highly competitive US market, and a move to expand its financial presence.

The questioner went on to say that in 1997, a £90 million trading loss was uncovered in NatWest Markets, the bank's investment bank, which many investors blamed on the investment bank's quality of management.

It was not difficult to see what the Treasury Select Committee were implying. Here was a failed bank led by a chairman with a background in zoology, a chief executive with no banking qualifications, and a head of the Risk Committee with a questionable track record at NatWest.

Whilst Sir Derek fielded the questions as best he could, it was not a convincing performance and the committee was clearly of the opinion that more could have been done in terms of anticipating what proved to be a major financial crisis.

John Thurso, a committee member, clearly somewhat frustrated by an unwillingness on the part of the board to admit responsibility, said at this juncture:

> Mr Applegarth, listening to you all here today, you sound like frightfully reasonable chaps who have been the ghastly victims of some financial Tsunami, yet the plain fact is you are in charge of the only bank that has had a run on it for 150 years. Do you actually accept you have done anything wrong?

In the ensuing responses Adam Applegarth put down the cause to be the speed, duration and the global nature of the liquidity freeze, heightened by the fact that Northern Rock did not have access to the same type of borrowing facilities that had been available for American banks from the US Reserve and for the European banks from the ECB.

This, to me, was a very significant factor. The implication here was that if Northern Rock could have availed itself of ECB funding (which was covert) none of this would have happened.

Liquidity

Under questioning, Adam Applegarth maintained that prior to the run there was two to three months worth of liquidity available to it, and that the request for a facility from the Bank of England was purely a standby measure. It was not intended to be drawn down, but once the run happened they had to.

Liquidity had actually increased since the start of the year (to £2.3 billion at the half year stage) and a £4.4 billion securitisation in May had been oversubscribed.

Questioned about the amount Northern Rock had borrowed from the Bank of England, he confirmed a figure of £13 billion. That indicated to me that the bulk of this sum probably represented the loss of deposits since the run.

Next came a very specific question which referred to Countrywide, a US mortgage bank, that had relied in a similar fashion to Northern Rock on short-term funding but chose to take out insurance against liquidity drying up:

Why didn't you take it out?

It transpired that on 17th August, about the time when Northern Rock was desperately trying to find a safe haven for its business, Countrywide was able to claim on its insurance and draw down $11.5 billion of committed credit lines. Applegarth's answer was that some insurance was in place but clearly it was inadequate to cope with the retail run. The reason why similar levels of insurance cover had not been put in place was because Northern Rock had a much broader funding platform than Countrywide's.

It was quite a surprise to me that the freezing up of the money markets – that inevitably proved to be the undoing of Northern Rock – was an insurable risk.

There was a further revelation when Applegarth said that a programme had been announced to sell commercial lending, its unsecured loan books and commercial buy to let books, as part of a strategy to slow lending growth and to create more liquidity. The sale of the commercial loan book (to Lehmans) had already taken place with the other two to happen later.

This was again news to us and until then we had assumed that the commercial buy to let business, which is what our office did, might be remaining with Northern Rock. It wasn't the best way to discover that effectively the whole business within which we worked, was earmarked to be sold off too.

Brand

The questioning then moved onto Northern Rock's brand:

Dr Ridley, would you agree that whatever else happens in the future that the good name of Northern Rock will be a casualty of your failures?

Put like that, this question was almost impossible to answer: if the Chairman of the bank admitted that the brand was dead, then indeed it would be.

Dr Ridley responded:

I would agree that there is some damage to the brand of Northern Rock and that is a matter of enormous distress to me and my colleagues…it is true to say that on the retail funding side the name Northern Rock is unlikely to continue. It is worth pointing out that on the mortgage lending side all our feedback from other brokers is that they know we are a good and responsible and careful lender, and that has not changed.

The questioner responded:

I think you are now accepting that Northern Rock is now finished as a name.

If I can pinpoint the exact moment that I, and my colleagues, finally realised that Northern Rock would not survive in its present form as a stand-alone company, it was then.

The run and lessons learnt

Adam Applegarth was questioned about what could have prevented the run on Northern Rock. Firstly, he said that he felt that if a takeover had been allowed to take place, and he could have announced an offer with a big retail brand, a run would have been avoided. He also said that he had a little difficulty understanding the moral hazard argument.

Secondly, he said that if a facility had existed in the UK, as it did in the USA and in Europe, where covert funding lines were available to Northern Rock, then again the run could have been averted. The reason for this was that Northern Rock was not regulated by the ECB as many other banks were, so the mechanism to do this did not exist.

Indeed, later in the questioning, Applegarth reiterated that a lesson learnt was that if Northern Rock had had more diverse retail funding, including funding through a branch in the Eurozone, that would have allowed access to the ECB facilities and not simply to be dependent on the UK facilities.

Thirdly, he said that had the leak not occurred, and an orderly announcement of the Bank of England facility had been made, with the appropriate levels of reassurance, a run on the bank may not have happened. He said:

As soon as you have language used in terms of "lender of the last resort" and "liquidity problems", that would frighten me as a retail customer.

Summary

Whilst the hearing covered other issues that I have not covered here – such as the role of the regulatory bodies, the balance between short and long-term funding, and the lead up to the run – these were the key revelations for me.

As was pointed out on a number of occasions, out of all the banks in both the UK and overseas they were the only ones in charge of a bank that had had a retail run and therefore had to take responsibility for it.

Not surprisingly, three days later on 19th October, Dr Matt Ridley resigned as Chairman of Northern Rock.

Trying to Find a Solution

At around this time, mid October to be precise, the mood started to change within the organisation. Whilst the departure of the Chairman came and went with hardly a comment from anyone, there was a significance to the event that was not lost on people. This was no longer a blip, it was now well and truly a rescue operation.

Staff morale

There was still a great deal of uncertainty about what would happen. I think everyone was fearful, to a greater or lesser degree, of losing their jobs, but still optimistic of a favourable outcome. So generally, staff were taking a wait-and-see approach.

One might imagine that we were getting weekly, if not daily, updates from within the organisation regarding ongoing events, but nothing could have been further from the truth. Whilst there were periodic internal communications, they were generally after the event; otherwise there was just silence.

Whilst it was tempting to continuously speculate about what was going to happen, it struck me that most people working for Northern Rock at the time kept their heads down and just got on with their jobs. Morale, in the circumstances, appeared on the surface to be reasonably high, albeit there was always this nagging uncertainty that the whole saga would ultimately end in tears. Most staff were putting a brave face on it.

Some, including myself, it has to be said, were taking steps to explore securing alternative employment, should that ultimately prove to be necessary to protect one's future. At that stage, however, I did not detect that the majority of Northern Rock staff had taken those steps, particularly those based in the north-east. This, I think, was because head office based staff did potentially have options to secure alternative roles within the company provided that it continued to exist in some shape or form.

Within Commercial Finance the situation was rather different, in that it was a more specialised business with only one outlet in the north-east. And as only a small part of Northern Rock's overall business, we did feel even more vulnerable than would normally be the case. After all, Adam Applegarth and the board had already made the decision to sell off the whole of the business managed by Commercial Finance, so even without Northern Rock's current plight there was quite a risk that, as an office, we might not have a long-term future.

The four possible outcomes for the Rock

At this juncture it was considered that there were four possible outcomes for Northern Rock as a business: administration, nationalisation, sale or takeover, and remaining independent.

Administration was the worst possible of all the potential outcomes. This would amount to the business being effectively wound up and its assets being sold off to repay its liabilities (including the Bank of England loan). That would be the end of Northern Rock as a business. In this scenario, there would be a heavy loss of jobs, which would cause enormous damage to the north-east economy. Politically, this appeared to be an option that the government did not want to pursue (thankfully), and for this reason was continuing to increase its loan support rather than let the bank go.

Nationalisation, which was also considered to be an unattractive option, would involve taking the bank into public ownership. Given the stigma attached to previously nationalised industries, for instance Railtrack, which were seen as disastrous failures, the government was keen to avoid going down this route.

Continuing as a stand-alone business, supported by the Bank of England, was looking increasingly unlikely since it was clear that the government wanted to see a swift resolution to the crisis.

A takeover was therefore the preferred and most likely option at this stage and, early in October, some potential candidates started to emerge. First up were two American investment groups, J.C. Flowers and Cerberus. Then, on 12th October, it became known that Sir Richard Branson's Virgin Group was putting together a financing package supported by debt funding from Citigroup up to a reported figure of £10 billion.

If successful, Virgin would take over the day-to-day management of the business and bring it under its Virgin Money brand, which already offered mortgages, credit cards and insurance services. It would retain Northern Rock's stock market listing.

This was considered internally to be a very positive move, in that Virgin was a recognised and respected brand. Also, early indications were that Virgin was looking to keep the business more or less intact. Northern Rock's share price was also responding positively to this potential bidding activity.

Internally, we speculated what the new brand would look like: *Northern Virgin* perhaps, or *Virgin of the Rock*?

However, a solution was starting to look more likely.

Reviewing the monitoring and regulation of banks – preventing another 9/14

Meanwhile, it was clear that efforts were being made to learn from the events of 9/14 (as it might be called). Efforts were being made to review both the regulatory framework surrounding the management of banks and also the system for guaranteeing deposits in the event of bank failure.

Sir Callum McCarthy and Hector Sants (respectively the Chairman and Chief Executive of the FSA) had appeared before the Treasury Select Committee on 9th October to defend the FSA's handling of the crisis. There was some tough questioning, particularly as Northern Rock had been rated by the FSA as "low risk". As Conservative MP, Michael Fallon, put it:

> You are dealing with a bank whose lending has quadrupled from £25 billion to £100 billion – it was taking one in five mortgages – and you were not doing a full assessment for three years.

It was agreed by the FSA that there had been lessons to be learnt from the crisis.

In the meantime Alistair Darling, the Chancellor, was telling MPs that he would introduce legislation in the New Year that would guarantee the savings and deposits held in all banks and building society accounts. Treasury officials said that savings up to £100,000 were expected to be covered (despite anticipated complaints from banks and insurers that the figure was too high). Mr Darling promised "comprehensive change" and went on to say:

> When problems do occur we need to have a system in place that is clear and reassures depositors. This regime would mean: depositors are insulated from a bank that has failed, greater compensation for them, and certainty their compensation can be paid out quickly.

The government had already introduced 100% protection for savings up to £35,000 after the run on Northern Rock. This was then extended to cover new savers.

At a level of £35,000, 96% of investors would be fully covered, so this figure was considered to afford adequate protection for the majority of savers.

On a side note: I spotted an article in the *Financial Times* that week in which it mentioned that Alistair Darling's own mortgage was in fact with Northern Rock.

Board changes and fear of job losses

Following the widely expected resignation of Dr Matt Ridley on 19th October, Bryan Sanderson, the former chairman of both Standard Chartered Bank and BUPA, was parachuted in to be appointed the new chairman of Northern Rock. Sanderson, who hails from County Durham, had his roots in the north-east and was a Sunderland supporter (not ideal for the chairman of a company that sponsored Newcastle United). In early interviews it was clear that his role was to find a solution to the Northern Rock problem which, in terms of its debt to the Bank of England, was a growing one. Sanderson was quoted as saying:

> We want to examine every option. The debt is not quite £20 billion just yet but it's getting there, and it could be as much as £25 billion by February.

Following Bryan Sanderson's appointment there was pressure for the rest of the board to quit. The press could not believe that the people who had been the architects of this horrendous situation were still in office. However, as far as Adam Applegarth was concerned, Sanderson saw his knowledge and experience of Northern Rock's mortgage business helpful in enabling him to understand the workings of the business. So, for the time being, Applegarth was staying.

There was also much speculation about potential job losses, particularly since Sanderson had said, in an interview with Radio 4's Today programme, that he could not guarantee that there would be no job losses because it depended on the outcome of the bids for the company and what the successful bidder might do.

These comments caused an outcry from the union, Unite:

> *Unite the union, is utterly appalled by the comments made by Bryan Sanderson. Unite has previously had assurances from Northern Rock that compulsory redundancies will be avoided. Vague comments such as those expressed by the Chairman merely result in further insecurity for the employees of the bank, at a time when they are already under massive strain.*

On 29th October, Adam Applegarth wrote an internal staff communication confirming that the intention was to deal with any required reduction in staff numbers by natural staff turnover and not through compulsory redundancy. As such, there was a continued freeze on recruitment in place. He also mentioned that the board was continuing to work closely with advisors and the authorities to develop the best way forward for Northern Rock, although he believed that the overall process might take some time to conclude.

He also made comment about the continued press coverage:

> *Much of the coverage is unhelpful, speculative in nature and obviously very unsettling for us all.*

The search for a buyer

It was becoming clear to us around then that there would not be a quick solution – this was going to be a marathon, not a sprint.

Early in November, Blackstone, one of Northern Rock's financial advisors, was understood to have sent a detailed sales memorandum to up to 50 parties potentially interested in bidding for the bank. Publicly, at this stage there were three potential bidders in the frame – J.C. Flowers, Cerberus and Virgin – who, we understood, were in the process of completing their due diligence. This memorandum set a two week deadline for any bids to be submitted.

In the meantime, bad news was emerging from the other side of the Atlantic where Citigroup declared substantial losses relating to the sub-prime crisis. This created shock waves in the financial markets. There were concerns about large potential write downs by UK banks – Barclays was forced to issue a statement denying rumours of a £10 billion write down as a result of losses relating to US sub-prime investments.

The credit crunch was hitting harder, and that was bad news for Northern Rock and its attempts to find a buyer with access to substantial funding (sufficient to repay the Bank of England borrowings).

Staff begin to leave

It also was claimed that Northern Rock had lost £14 billion in retail deposits since the run, despite the government guarantees to depositors that were in place. This figure was denied by the company as a substantial overestimate, although clearly a "silent run" had taken place over the weeks and months following the initial run in September that had eroded its deposit base.

Around this time I recall seeing a headline in one of the daily tabloids headed:

Zombie fear for stricken bank

which was suggesting that Northern Rock was now in a zombie-like state in that it was effectively doing little new lending and more or less going through the motions, just waiting for some sort of resolution to the crisis.

That is, more or less, how it was. Certainly in my division of commercial finance. And, not surprisingly, staff had started to leave. The Bromley office had closed down completely, following the departure of its two lending managers. Key staff in other offices were leaving too and were not being replaced.

These were very difficult times.

The Rock continues to dominate the media

On 6th November, Mervyn King, Governor of the Bank of England, was interviewed by Radio 4 about the events leading up to the run. The cru x of what is called the "moral hazard" argument was that facilitating a bail out of a bank that had pursued a risky lending strategy, without penalty, would have been the wrong thing to do in that it would have encouraged other lenders in the future to take similar risks, which could potentially have even worse consequences further down the line.

On 9th November, BBC2's The Money Programme had a feature on the Northern Rock crisis titled "Run on the Bank: Northern Crock". The media interest in the Northern Rock crisis continued unabated and the company's management, the FSA, the Bank of England and the Chancellor, were all facing criticism for their respective roles in the wake of Northern Rock's collapse.

On 11th November, a new serious bidder emerged. This was Luqman Arnold, who was the former head of Abbey National and who turned it round prior to selling it to Banco Santander. Arnold's investment company was called Olivant. This news was very encouraging: a fourth bidder – it raised the prospects of a bidding war.

Soon afterwards, stories appeared in the press relating to the sale of £2.6 million in Northern Rock shares by Adam Applegarth in August 2006 and January 2007. Whilst this was headline grabbing stuff – and there was much play on the fact that these funds had been used to support a luxury lifestyle – the timing of the share sales were such that he clearly did not sell at a time when he knew the company was in trouble.

Whilst the fall of Northern Rock was undoubtedly a big story, the scale of the media coverage on anything connected with it was staggering. And any opportunity to take a swipe at the Chief Executive and the board was taken with gusto.

Applegarth and other directors resign

It is difficult to say whether this further adverse publicity had anything to do with it, but on 16th November there was an announcement that Adam Applegarth was resigning, but for the moment would stay on to help manage the expected sale of Northern Rock.

This was part of a wider boardroom reshuffle where Sir Derek Wanless, Nichola Pease, Adam Fenwick and Rosemary Radcliffe all retired as non-executive directors. The company announcement said:

> The streamlining of the board is intended to assist with a smooth and rapid decision making process around the strategic review of the company's options, which is currently in progress.

It is a feature of the flexibility of the English language that a desperate attempt to rescue a company from the impact of the largest banking collapse in living memory can be called a "strategic review".

The outgoing non-execs were being replaced by John Devaney, who was chairman of National Air Traffic Services, and Simon Laffin, a private equity expert and previously the chief financial officer of Safeway.

The media reaction to the shake-up was that it should have happened much earlier. The retention of the services of Adam Applegarth was widely criticised.

The Preferred Solution – A Takeover

From my perspective the crisis had now taken on an impetus of its own, in that Northern Rock's future was now in the hands of people who had had no prior involvement with the company before its spectacular crash. Only two months had passed but the game was up and it was now a case of trying to make the best out of a bad job.

Around this time I attended the last formal meeting for the commercial finance arm of Northern Rock and there was very much an air of resignation to it. The opinion was that the business would be sold and it was now just a case of who to and when.

My Commercial Finance Manager, Graham, resigned to take up a new role with the commercial arm of a building society. Naturally, he was not going to be replaced, but then at this time there was virtually no new lending being done.

Virgin becomes the preferred bidder

On 26th November it was announced that the board had decided that Virgin was the preferred bidder for Northern Rock and accelerated discussions would commence. The key points were as follows:

- Northern Rock would be rebranded Virgin, retain its stock market listing subject to the relevant rules, and would continue without any break-up of the business.

- No material reduction in jobs was intended and the business would continue to be operated from the north-east of England.

- The intention was for Virgin to capitalise on the strength of its brand, with the introduction of additional top management, and experience from the Virgin Money business bringing the business a renewed confident future for the benefit of all stakeholders.

- The intention was that the Northern Rock Foundation would continue to participate in the profits of the company.

Whilst the announcement made the point that there was no certainty that the discussions would lead to a transaction taking place, we very much viewed this as being the solution to the problem and many staff were quite looking forward to the prospect of working under the Virgin banner. In addition, it was announced that the Treasury was going to maintain the existing guarantee arrangement to savers.

So, on the day of this announcement, 26th November 2007, I fully expected that we were nearing the final chapter.

However, the "strategic review" – which was supposed to be exploring all available options and then choosing the best one – was estimated to take until February 2008; so it became fairly clear that the process was not as straightforward as one might have imagined.

At this stage, the Bank of England loan to Northern Rock was reportedly at a figure of around £26 billion and rising, which was in itself an issue that was causing considerable adverse publicity – and adverse press publicity was certainly something that Northern Rock was extremely keen to avoid at this time. I had heard that executives had been advised not to use their mobile phones when travelling publicly in case their conversations were overheard and leaked to the press.

Towards the end of November, managers were sent a note making it clear that they should not pay for, or partially pay for, any bill for a staff festive event using company funds on the basis that we could be accused of "abusing tax-payers' money". That was a pretty hard pill to swallow given the effort the staff of Northern Rock had put in, particularly over the last three months of the year. But the environment was such that some of the more unscrupulous members of the press were prepared to find any angle they could to generate a good story.

Although at this stage Virgin was the preferred bidder, there were still four bidders having talks with the Northern Rock board: Virgin, Olivant, J.C. Flowers, and Cerberus.

In the meantime it emerged that two hedge funds, RAB Capital and SRM Global Investments, had been building up their stakes in Northern Rock and by now owned about 17% of the business between them. SRM was reported as having increased its stake to 9.1% in a move designed to ensure that the hedge fund had a say in determining any future owner for Northern Rock. RAB Capital owned 6.7% of Northern Rock.

Virgin or Olivant?

As major shareholders, the hedge funds were clearly going to support the bid that gave the highest return to shareholders, and their view was that the Virgin bid was less favourable than Olivant's in that regard.

The Virgin consortium proposal involved injecting £1.3 billion of cash plus the Virgin Money business – which it valued at £250 million – into Northern Rock. Half the cash would be supplied by Virgin and half would come from a rights issue to existing investors at 25p per ordinary share.

The consortium would be left with up to 55% of Northern Rock, which would keep its stock market listing. Critics said shareholders would pay to refinance the business and be left with only 45% of the company. Virgin said the plan was designed so that shareholders could share in the bank's revival.

Virgin would charge Northern Rock for the use of the Virgin brand, as it does with other businesses in which it invests. (Sir Richard Branson would receive at least £255 million over the following 30 years for licensing the Virgin brand name to NTL after selling Virgin Mobile to the company.)

Jayne-Anne Gadhia, the Chief Executive of Virgin Money, admitted that the deal for shareholders was "the most contentious point", but said she believed the alternative was that they and other stakeholders would be left with nothing. According to her:

> We are giving shareholders the opportunity to participate in the upside.

Luqman Arnold's Olivant, on the other hand, proposed buying about 15% of Northern Rock in a rights issue at a discount to the prevailing share price and installing Mr Arnold as chief executive. It believed that Northern Rock needed a maximum of about £600 million of extra equity and argued that its proposal would not dilute shareholders' interests to anything like the extent that the Virgin plan would.

Olivant said that it and the shareholders would profit if Mr Arnold turned the business round. It also said that its idea could be implemented more quickly than Virgin's and that speed would be important to salvage Northern Rock.

Virgin would repay £11 billion of Northern Rock's debt to the Bank of England upfront and the rest (about another £11 billion) by the end of 2010. Olivant proposed repaying between £10 billion and £11 billion straight away and settling up with the Bank and the Treasury within about two years.

Broker Keefe, Bruyette & Woods estimated that the Olivant offer of £800 million of new equity diluted its estimated book value per share from 448p to 224p. Far better than Virgin's 52p bid.

On 7th December, buyout firm J.C. Flowers withdrew from the auction to buy Northern Rock. It had found it "impossible" to construct a deal that would deliver the required value for Northern Rock shareholders alongside its own profitability criteria. With no formal bid in sight from Cerberus this was now effectively a two horse race, with five major shareholders (with a 23% combined stake in the company) said to be backing the Olivant bid.

The difficulty both bidders were having was actually raising the funds required to repay half of the Bank of England loan because of the credit crunch. Key potential funders RBS, Deutsche Bank and Citibank were reported to not be prepared to sign any deal in 2007 whilst the credit crunch continued.

In addition, any successful bid was going to have to be contingent on the Bank of England continuing to provide support, possibly for a number of years.

Applegarth finally leaves, and ejection from the FTSE100

On 13th December, Adam Applegarth finally left Northern Rock and Andy Kuipers, previously shunted off the board, was appointed chief executive in his place. Adam Applegarth wrote an emotional letter to the staff of Northern Rock.

Whilst he has been much maligned by the press throughout the crisis, I think he genuinely gave his all for the company he had spent all of his working life with. He said that he was heartbroken at having to leave Northern Rock in these circumstances and I believe that he genuinely was.

It was later reported that he received a pay-off of £760,000. Although this amount was said to be considerably less than the package that would have been available to him had he left the company under normal circumstances, this didn't cut much ice with the press who would have liked to have seen him leave with nothing.

At the same time Northern Rock was ejected from the FTSE100 index having joined it in September 2001. Once commanding a market value of £5.3 billion, it was now worth an estimated £417 million, less than 8% of its previous value.

Into 2008, and the hedge funds flex their muscles

Meanwhile, behind the scenes there appeared to be a battle emerging between the shareholders led by SRM Global and RAB Capital and the company. On 21st December, Northern Rock agreed to hold an emergency meeting for shareholders to discuss its sale process on 15th January. It also emerged early in the New Year that any consideration for nationalisation of Northern Rock would have to be at a fair price. Failure to do so would result in a class action being taken against the government in the European Court of Human Rights.

On 12th January it was reported that Northern Rock had agreed to sell £2.2 billion (being 2%) of its mortgage assets to US investment bank JPMorgan. The price represented a 2.25% premium to the value of the assets and confirmed that the funds would be used to pay back some of the £25 billion of emergency loans it had been given by the Bank of England.

On 13th January a feature article appeared in the *Sunday Mail* which clearly would cause embarrassment to Northern Rock's top management. It was entitled:

Double pay deal for Rock bosses

The article reported that senior staff at Northern Rock had received secret bonuses doubling their salaries – at a time when the bank was being propped up by billions of pounds of taxpayers' money. (I should mention that I was certainly not one of them.)

It was reported that in a letter to senior staff on 20th December, Chief Executive Andy Kuipers said the bank's board of directors had agreed "an enhanced remuneration package" for employees deemed:

essential to our continuing excellent operational performance

Kuipers said they would receive a bonus amounting to a quarter of their gross annual salary every three months – effectively doubling their pay if they were paid the bonus for a year. The arrangement could be withdrawn only with three months' written notice, so the employees were guaranteed at least six months' extra pay. The payouts were capped at £25,000 per quarter and took effect from that month. The formula meant that some staff – those earning £100,000 or less – could double their pay.

Northern Rock defended these payments saying:

They are deemed essential to the immediate and ongoing stability and operational effectiveness of the company. The board considers this to be responsible and prudent business practice, particularly given our current situation, and is a matter on which the tripartite authorities have been fully appraised.

Nevertheless, this had an adverse impact on the morale of staff who were hugely disappointed that such large bonuses had been agreed just one month after being told not to buy staff drinks at Christmas for fear of adverse publicity.

Whilst the events were not connected, the next day, 14th January, I resigned my position at Northern Rock. I was just one of many who had left Commercial Finance. Indeed, by this time it was clear that such were the extent of Northern Rock's difficulties we were being encouraged to secure our futures with another employer if we could.

On 15th January about 600 Northern Rock shareholders attended a key meeting with management. Bryan Sanderson, the Chairman, stood up to give his opening address. He raised a laugh by describing his job as the "second toughest job in Newcastle" – a thinly veiled reference to the football manager's job at Newcastle

United which had just been acquired by Kevin Keegan. He paid tribute to Northern Rock's employees, for working extremely professionally in these difficult times. "We've benefited from a Geordie backs-to-the-wall mentality." On the issue of rescuing the bank he said that the board was still on track to complete its review in February.

He moved onto the two shareholders RAB Capital and SRM Global, who had forced the meeting and had tabled four resolutions that would prevent the bank's board from selling assets or issuing new shares. He said that these additional restrictions were more likely to hamper the board's ability to rescue the bank than help it.

In the event only one of the resolutions was passed, which had little impact on the board's powers. This was more an opportunity for angry shareholders to say their piece.

No end in sight

Very little news was materialising about the sale process. It appeared to be taking an awfully long time to resolve. The board was trying to produce its own rescue plan, which was something I believe the majority of staff and shareholders were keen to support.

The longer this uncertainty went on the worse position the business was in. Business levels were very low. At its peak Northern Rock was processing 1,000 mortgage applications per day. This had reduced to 80. I heard one report that staff were leaving Northern Rock at a rate approaching 100 per week. There was a recruitment freeze so it struck me that, if this was true, it would not take long to get the staff numbers down. There was also a lot of redeployment between Head Office departments as mortgage business fell away and the push to sell savings products increased. As regards Commercial Finance, virtually all lending staff had left and the business was being managed by operational support staff.

I was still working my notice period for Northern Rock but, frankly, there was nothing to do.

There was still talk of nationalisation, although most people believed that this was an action the government wished to avoid.

On 21st January, Chancellor Alistair Darling announced a plan to convert Northern Rock's £25 billion Bank of England loan into bonds before selling them to investors – a plan devised by bankers Goldman Sachs. The bonds would be guaranteed by the government to speed up a private sale.

Potential bidders were given until 4th February to come forward with rescue proposals based on the Treasury's plans.

Northern Rock shares rose 42% on the news because it looked at that stage that a private sector sale was still likely, and probably on better terms for shareholders than originally thought.

The deadline for offers came and went but only Sir Richard Branson's Virgin Group and Northern Rock's own board made rescue proposals for the bank. Olivant pulled out, reportedly because the government wanted its £25 billion of direct loans to Northern Rock repaid within three years.

Virgin abandoned a commitment to no redundancies because government-backed bonds to be issued by Northern Rock had to be repaid within three years and this particular issue created a lot of concern. Northern Rock's current management, which submitted a rival plan, said it would fight to prevent job cuts.

The situation continued to drag on, with indications that the government were not entirely happy with the initial rescue proposals and was looking for improved bids from both remaining parties.

Leaving the Rock

On Monday 11th February 2008, I finally left Northern Rock after almost three years with the company to take up a new position with a building society.

I drove into Leeds to say a final goodbye to my remaining team there and to hand in various pieces of equipment including my laptop, printer and mobile phone. As had been the case for some time they had very little ongoing work to do. The official line on any new commercial lending enquiries was to say that at the present time Northern Rock was not in a position to offer competitive terms. There was simply no desire to provide new commercial loans to borrowers and the business was basically treading water.

I drove the 100 miles or so to Northern Rock's head office in Gosforth, Newcastle, to return my company car. It was very sad walking towards the reception desk at the front of the building to see the place so quiet. I recall from previous visits that the building had always had a vibrant feel to it, bustling with large numbers of people passing through it. Now it looked and felt like a ghost town.

The lady I met with to deposit my keys was – as always – very friendly and wished me all the best in my new job. She remarked that she was being inundated with cars as an increasing number of employees were leaving the company. She was expecting another six new leavers that morning who would, in due course, be returning their company cars.

There was clearly a lot of concern within head office about job losses. Business volumes had shrunk to such a low level that there was simply not enough work to do. Many of these surplus employees were either seconded to other departments or engaged on project work. There was a lot of effort being made to attract deposits by offering attractive savings products. Rather sadly, had such efforts been made in the years prior to the crash Northern Rock's funding model might not have been so vulnerable. However, efforts to grow the deposit book were not without challenges.

The previous week a savings product offering a gross interest rate of 6.95% had to be withdrawn following complaints from competitors that the availability of financial support from the government was giving it an unfair advantage. The product was repriced at an interest rate of 6.5%.

The people I spoke to on the reception desk as I left agreed that redundancies now looked inevitable. At that stage an announcement was still expected from the Chancellor regarding which bid had been successful: either that from the Virgin Group or the in-house solution led by Northern Rock's new board of directors.

One said that if the worst happened and her job went she would probably get a job at Tesco or somewhere similar; and since she was shortly due to receive her Northern Rock lump sum pension this would be sufficient to keep her going. What had always struck me about the reactions of employees within the company was an almost matter of fact resignation that things had gone badly wrong but there was nothing much they could do about it and so the best thing was to simply carry on as normal. People were remarkably cheerful considering the circumstances.

Indeed, the day-to-day routine, by and large, seemed to continue as normal. I was amazed by the number of people I spoke to who just took the view that they would wait to see what happened. Most of them had been with the company a long time and since redundancy payments were geared to length of service they were hoping that a decent lump sum could be coming their way if the worst happened.

Nevertheless, people were leaving Northern Rock at quite a high rate. The situation was reminiscent to me of the sinking of the Titanic. Whilst in some areas of the ship there was a mad scramble to get off, there were others who were happily sitting at the bar watching the band play.

As regards Commercial Finance, the mood was somewhat different.

The Commercial Finance division

Commercial Finance as a business had already lost some lending managers following the announcement of the sale of its commercial loan book to Lehmans in June 2007. Two offices (Bristol and Bromley) were closed down, leaving six remaining. I had joked at the time that this was the only expanding business I knew that was closing down branches. Downsizing is not the best way to get one's staff motivated.

The sale of the commercial loan book had been a universally unpopular decision. Whilst the intention was for us to continue to source new loans under the Northern Rock banner to be, at some stage, sold on to Lehmans, we doubted whether this would work effectively. This concept had worked for Northern Rock's sub-prime mortgage business but, frankly, sub-prime borrowers were not particularly choosey about who they took the money from as they got it. Commercial borrowers like to know who they are dealing with, and acting as an agency for an American bank with no presence in the UK was not the best way to attract their business.

There were those, including myself, who were prepared to give it a try, but we felt that sourcing commercial loans for Lehmans and developing residential buy to let business was not what we joined Northern Rock to do. Almost all of the Commercial Lending Managers left in the business, including myself, had been talking to other banks.

For some, deciding whether or not to leave a company can be an agonising decision. In my case the events on 14th September made the decision for me. I knew that the organisation would never recover from that and I also knew that I would have no credibility in the commercial arena whatsoever after such a high-profile collapse. The brand had been very seriously damaged.

After the run there had been a total freeze on recruitment and so when a lending manager left there was no replacement. By the end of 2007, a business which, at its peak, had twenty lending managers was now down to just nine and, by February 2008, there were only a handful of lending managers left. The remaining offices housed only support staff and almost all of these were actively looking for other jobs. Indeed, by the end of the year I was getting a clear message that anyone who was not looking for alternative employment had not read the signals properly.

By that time the working relationship between Northern Rock and Lehmans had significantly deteriorated. Hardly any new business was being sourced and there was no appetite to lend given the extent of the Bank of England loans. There were virtually no new enquiries.

The mood in the offices was surreal. Nothing was happening. The telephone might not ring for three hours. The biggest challenge the remaining offices had was finding enough work to do to fill the day. Some staff brought books and magazines into work to read. The usual monthly meetings had all been cancelled – there was no longer anything to talk about. Everyone was simply waiting for an announcement as to what was going to happen to the company.

I reflected on how long it had taken to turn around the commercial finance office at Leeds and the effort it took to get there. At the start of 2007 everything had looked promising. I had a really good team, lots of new business coming in and an expectation of a record year. Now all that had been destroyed. Although I was leaving Northern Rock it very much felt as if Northern Rock had left me.

As I left Northern Rock's head office building at Gosforth I could not help but feel that there was an air of sadness, indeed resignation about the place. It was like witnessing a slow death. The new curved tower which was to increase office space at the head office complex still stood uncompleted. Now, I imagined, the existing building was going to be far too big for what was going to remain of the business.

It was now almost five months after the September run and, looking back, what I had witnessed had been a steady decline, where initial hopes of a quick resolution and a return to normality had given way to resignation and desperation. I think that people just wanted some resolution.

As it turned out resolution was not far away, but not in the form the company's employees had anticipated.

Nationalisation Announced

At 3.30pm on Sunday 17th February, Sky News broke the story that the Chancellor of the Exchequer was due to make a press statement a little later to announce the nationalisation of Northern Rock.

I was watching a 5th Round FA cup tie at the time, but quickly turned over to Sky News.

Whilst I had always recognised that nationalisation was a real option I felt, as did most people I spoke to, that this was not an option the government wanted to take. With two offers on the table and under review (from Virgin and the in-house consortium) the timing of this announcement took me by surprise.

The media were also taken by surprise. As were the shareholders. I recall seeing somebody from the Northern Rock Shareholder's Association being interviewed, and he clearly saw this as being a complete disaster for the company, shareholders and staff.

The Chancellor's announcement – 17th February

The statement was delivered at 4.15pm by Alistair Darling. He said that a review of the two proposals had been completed and that neither provided, in the view of the Treasury, sufficient protection for the taxpayer, which – as far as the government was concerned – was the primary aim.

As such, it had been decided that the government needed to step in to protect the taxpayers' interests and it was proposed that there would be a temporary period of public ownership in order to put the bank back onto a stable footing. The Bank of England and the FSA had been fully consulted and were both in agreement with the move.

As far as the operation of Northern Rock was concerned it would be open for business as usual on Monday. Depositors' money would remain absolutely secure and the government guarantees currently in place would continue.

He stressed that it was not the intention of the government to get involved in the day-to-day running of Northern Rock and that it would be run at arms length. He announced the appointment of Ron Sandler (ex-Lloyd's of London boss) as executive chair to run the bank.

Legislation would be introduced on the following day (February 18th) with a view to the proposals being agreed by parliament. The reason for the announcement taking place then (on a Sunday) was that the announcement needed to be made prior to the stock market opening on Monday morning.

During the announcement the Chancellor took the opportunity to recap on the background to the present position.

He referred to the problems in the sub-prime mortgage market the previous year that started in the US and then spread to Europe and Asia, with banks extremely reluctant to lend to each other in the autumn. As a result of this market turbulence a number of companies ran into difficulties in the US and in Germany; $100 billion had been written off the books of financial institutions globally since the summer.

He mentioned that in Germany, a number of banks had experienced difficulties and received support; the previous week the German government announced a further €1 billion of support to IKB. The authorities had to take action to preserve financial stability in countries right across the world.

Because of its particular business model, Northern Rock, the previous summer, had found it increasingly difficult and then impossible to raise the billions of pounds it needed to finance its business. For financial stability reasons, it was decided that it was right to support Northern Rock to allow it to continue operating. It was right to protect depositors' money and to protect the wider financial system.

In agreeing to that support, the government had three objectives.

Firstly, financial stability. In the then prevailing conditions, there was a serious risk that other parts of the banking system in the UK could have been destabilised. It was right and necessary for the government to intervene because of the need to preserve financial stability in the system. That support was successful and prevented further contagion.

Secondly, the government was also determined to safeguard depositors' money and action was taken to put in place guarantee arrangements which had been successful. None of the guarantees have been called and therefore there has been no cost to the taxpayer.

The third objective was protecting the interests of the taxpayer. The Chancellor said he believed it was right to allow the board and shareholders to explore every opportunity to find a private sector solution, subject to not increasing taxpayer costs. While in September and October uncertainty in the market made it difficult to attract potential buyers, in November and December the board of Northern Rock received a number of expressions of interest.

In testing them it became clear that no institution was prepared to make an offer for Northern Rock without some form of public support because of prevailing market conditions. That is why the government was prepared to consider a backstop guarantee arrangement to allow the board and shareholders to explore a private sector solution, provided that the terms and conditions were acceptable and met the principles set out.

In order to provide certainty for all interested parties and meet state aid rules, a solution had to be found by 17th March, an EU imposed deadline. It was not possible, nor would it have been desirable, to go beyond that time. The two detailed proposals received, one from the Virgin consortium and one from Northern Rock directors, had to be considered alongside temporary public ownership.

Both proposals involved a degree of risk for taxpayers and very significant implicit subsidy from the Treasury. This involved a payment to it at below the market rate for the continuation of the government guarantee arrangements and for the financing that would have to be put in place by the Bank of England.

He acknowledged that each proposal had its pros and cons. The Virgin proposal, for instance, would have brought a new brand and management. However, the taxpayer would only have seen any share of the private sector's return if the value of the business to its investors had reached at least £2.7 billion. The Northern Rock board's proposal would have involved a similar level of subsidy. But it had other disadvantages, compared with Virgin, including: it would bring in less new capital, provide less buffer protecting the taxpayer from risk, and the business would have been dependent on government guarantees for new retail deposits for longer.

He concluded that a subsidy on the scale required would not, in the government's judgment, provide best value for money for the taxpayer, in circumstances where the private sector rather than the taxpayer would secure the vast majority of the value created over the period ahead. By contrast, under public ownership the government would secure the entire proceeds from the future sale of the business in return for bearing the risks in periods of market uncertainty.

In short, the taxpayers' interests, in his view, were better protected in public ownership than through either of the private sector options in that under public ownership the government would secure, for the benefit of the taxpayer, the entire proceeds from the future sale of the business.

He then announced the next steps, which were for shares in Northern Rock to be suspended before the opening of the London Stock Exchange and a bill to be published to bring Northern Rock into temporary public ownership. As regards shareholders, an independent adjudicator was to be appointed to assess the value of the shares, but on the basis that the Bank of England support was not in place. Northern Rock Foundation, its charitable arm, would be guaranteed a minimum income of £15 million per year in 2008, 2009 and 2010. He also said that Ron Sandler, the newly appointed bank chairman, would be visiting Newcastle on Monday morning to meet staff and their representatives.

Ron Sandler questioned

Questions were put to Ron Sandler; his response was along the lines that the intention was to revitalise the bank and to continue to operate on a normal commercial basis, ultimately delivering the benefits back to the taxpayer.

He was quick to stress the strengths: excellent work force, a track record of innovation, leading products, etc.

He said he would need to take stock of where business was then. Northern Rock had grown rapidly in recent years and his intention was to return it to a more sustainable size. This was therefore going to be a new chapter for Northern Rock. It still had a key role however, in the north-east as an employer and through the Foundation. The strategy and day-to-day running of the bank would be determined by local management teams.

He reiterated that it had been entirely right to see if there was a market-led solution, however it was clear that one could not be achieved. Sandler said:

I believe that when market conditions improve it will be possible to return it back into private ownership. However this was a highly unusual period and in the face of such uncertainty it was better to get 100% of any improved value than pursue the solutions on offer.

He was asked about job losses; not surprisingly he steered well clear of that debate saying:

We will have to reach a judgement on how to run Northern Rock and will be meeting first of all with management and staff.

Reaction to the announcement

Immediately after the announcement, Angela Knight of the British Bankers' Association was interviewed on Sky TV. She was keen to see a plan to run the bank and a plan for the future before making too much by way of comment.

She said that the UK had not been the only country with this type of problem and that we needed to look at other countries where there had been difficulties with other banks over the credit crunch and how those problems had been handled.

The interviewer asked:

Why has it taken so long for a resolution to take place, people think it is looking messy?

She replied:

I agree with you actually.

She was not prepared to criticise the government over the handling of the crisis, but did say that action should have been taken earlier and confidentiality should have been in place. There was a lot that needed to change and future prevention was the key.

I took this as meaning that she believed the government had not handled it that well.

George Osborne (Shadow Chancellor) was rather more critical:

This is the day when Labour's reputation for economic competence died. Gordon Brown has dithered his way to the disaster of nationalisation. Now the taxpayer will bear the full risk of lending £100 billion of mortgages in an uncertain housing market. We will not back nationalisation. We will not help Gordon Brown take this country back to the 1970s.

He also said that nationalisation would do enormous reputational damage to the UK as a financial institution, and that, instead, there should have been a Bank of England led reconstruction.

Sir Richard Branson expressed his disappointment with the decision. He said that nationalisation was "not the right answer" for Northern Rock and maintained that the Virgin Group had tried its best to save "Northern Rock and the jobs of the staff".

In a statement, Sir Richard said:

We believe nationalisation is not the right answer and that a commercial solution would have been the best way forward.

Representatives of the shareholders were also very unhappy. Robin Ashby from Northern Rock Small Shareholders, said he was "shocked" and "appalled" at the government's decision.

Mr Ashby, who backed the in-house management team bid, slammed the move saying:

It was part of the mismanagement of the whole Northern Rock saga.

My reaction was equally one of shock. Whilst nationalisation had always been positioned as an option, the expectation was that one of the bids would be accepted and that Northern Rock would be bought out with shareholders having some sort of a stake in its future. Nationalisation was likely to leave the shareholders with next to nothing, particularly if the basis of valuation was that the Bank of England support was not available. As a shareholder myself – like many employees and ex-employees of Northern Rock

– I realised that the personal financial cost of this could be substantial.

However, my other reaction was one of great sadness, because I saw this as the final chapter in Northern Rock's history as a major UK bank. It is inconceivable that it will ever return to anything like its former glory.

As one might expect, the next day the media had a field day.

This was clearly going to be a huge embarrassment for the government. There were angry reactions from shareholders and from the staff unions who were seeking urgent talks about potential job losses. The credibility of Alistair Darling and Gordon Brown was brought into question, as indeed was the way in which the whole crisis had been handled by the government from start to finish. The view was that this had been an unmitigated disaster and, if nationalisation was the right solution, the decision should have been made much earlier.

At 3.30pm, on Monday 18th February 2008, Alistair Darling, the Chancellor of the Exchequer, stood up from the government benches in the House of Commons and said:

> With permission, Mr Speaker, I would like to make a statement on Northern Rock.

What Went Wrong?

In this chapter I try to summarise the major factors that caused the crisis at Northern Rock.

There was no single cause, but rather a number of factors which, combined together, proved to be absolutely disastrous. Indeed, it seems that almost everything that could have gone wrong did so.

Cause 1 – Northern Rock's business model

Northern Rock's business model has been described as many things from extreme to reckless. What exactly does that mean?

Firstly, there were many good things about the way Northern Rock operated its business. It had good products, it was very competitive on price, it retained its customers well, kept its costs low and had a good quality loan book with an arrears record running at half the industry average. In addition, it did not retain any sub-prime (low quality) mortgages on its balance sheet.

The area of Northern Rock's business model that has attracted strong criticism is how it funded its rapidly increasing mortgage lending activity.

The problem was that between its demutulisation in 1997 and the end of December 2006, Northern Rock's deposits hardly more than doubled from £10 billion to £23 billion. However, there had been a sixfold increase in its mortgage lending over the same period.

That meant that by the end of 2006, retail deposits as a proportion of Northern Rock's total liabilities and equity, fell from 63% in 1997, to 22% in 2006. This was low. For comparison, Alliance & Leicester's proportion was 43% and Bradford & Bingley's was 49%.

Because Northern Rock could not hope to fund its ambitious mortgage growth targets by increasing its retail deposits, it began borrowing increasing amounts of funds from the wholesale money markets on a short-term basis. Periodically, it would then parcel up mortgages and use them as security for further funding (the process known as securitisation).

This funding model is known as "originate and distribute" and is used by many other lenders. In 2006, Northern Rock raised 43% of its funds in this way.

What was unique about Northern Rock's business model was that it was more reliant on its ability to raise wholesale funds in the money markets and to securitise its mortgages than other mortgage lenders.

The model had worked well over the years but that was because market conditions had been stable and raising funds in the money markets had not proved to be a problem. However, in its April 2007 Financial Stability Report, the Bank of England had identified that there was a potential risk that markets might become less liquid as a result of the American sub-prime crisis.

What has come under great scrutiny is how the board of Northern Rock, at that time, reacted to this potentially increased risk, at a time when it was continuing to expand its mortgage lending at full throttle.

Internally there was no message or warning that growth should be slowed. Internal communications talked only of going for growth and achieving ambitious lending targets. Northern Rock's management had considered that in the event of the money markets tightening up there would be a "flight to quality", in that its better quality mortgage assets would attract what limited funding there was. Also, because Northern Rock had a range of funding options – in that it sourced funds worldwide – a complete closure of all money market and securitisation funding was simply not anticipated.

Unfortunately these assumptions proved to be false.

After 9th August 2007, when the money markets froze, Northern Rock had got itself into a position whereby it was running out of money. Its strategy of borrowing short and lending long had caught up with it and the bank needed help.

In terms of who was to blame, the House of Commons Treasury Committee concluded that the directors of Northern Rock were the principal authors of the problems the bank encountered after 9th August. It described the bank's business model as high risk, reckless and with an over reliance on short- and medium-term funding.

In addition, the directors failed to arrange additional insurance or a standby facility to cover the risk of the money markets drying up. Fundamentally, it is the role of management to ensure that a bank remains solvent and able to meet its commitments. In that regard the board of directors failed in its duty.

These problems were well hidden, in that the majority of employees, such as myself, assumed that the board had managed Northern Rock's funding lines prudently. The same could not be said of many market analysts, who had been encouraging investors to sell, pointing to flaws in Northern Rock's business model.

As I have said, there was definitely a contradiction at the time between what was being said by the market and what was being said by the company's directors. It was not until 13th September that we learned the truth.

Cause 2 – The dash for growth

The sheer scale of Northern Rock's growth did not, in itself, cause its problems. However, continuing a high rate of growth at a time when the market was turning did – particularly when combined with an extreme business model.

When Adam Applegarth was pressed on this point at the House of Commons Treasury Select Committee hearing, he maintained that as a result of the Financial Stability Report the board had implemented a new strategy to slow down its lending growth:

> On the back of the warning signs, you saw us announce a change in strategy with the interim results that were slowing down the rate of asset growth, which we had done from the third month of this year, and we announced that we were going to sell various higher risk asset books on the balance sheet. We completed the sale of the commercial loan book, which is about a £2 billion loan book, over three stages, with the first stage actually taking place after 9 August.

However, if there was a policy in place to slow down the rate of growth from March 2007, it does not appear to be one that had been communicated to the staff. There was no relaxing of sales targets and no internal briefings that I was aware of outlining a change of policy. Indeed, in an internal publication covering the half year results to 30th June 2007, Adam Applegarth said:

> Despite the headwind and all of the criticism levelled at us, we have announced expected growth in underlying profits of around 15%. But we do not manage the business for the short term, we look 2-3 years out. This is why we deliberately continued volume lending. Even though we are squeezed in the short term, our excellence in customer service and retention means we can look forward to keeping customers for several years, re-pricing their loans more than once.

That statement did not suggest to me that Northern Rock was looking to slow down its rate of growth. Indeed, it suggests a strategy to con tinue volume lending as part of a longer term expansion strategy on the basis that any short term squeeze will rectify itself further down the line.

It is worth looking at some of the numbers reported by the company for the first half of 2007 compared to the 2006 first half results. Gross lending up by 31%, net lending up by 47%, gross residential mortgage lending up by 37%, net residential lending up by 59%, total assets up by 28%, retail balances (deposits) up 12%, gross mortgage market share of 9.7%, net mortgage market share of 19%.

These figures do not give the impression of a company in the process of consolidation.

Indeed, the gross mortgage market share figures indicate that in the first half of 2007, one out of every ten mortgages in the UK was provided by Northern Rock.

Whilst Northern Rock's business model was the main reason for its initial problems, the rate of its expansion merely accelerated the rate at which those difficulties occurred. Even the sale of the commercial loan book and the granting by the FSA of its Basel II waiver failed to provide the cushion needed to avoid its difficulties.

My view is that the management of Northern Rock were convinced that the rate of expansion enjoyed over the previous ten years could be continued and that the company's strategy and business model were both robust enough to support this growth. Had a more conservative approach been adopted, the sheer speed with which its difficulties occurred may have slowed this process and allowed the board more time to engineer a solution.

Cause 3 – Ineffective regulatory controls

The FSA has already acknowledged that there were failings in its regulation of Northern Rock in the months immediately preceding the September run.

In its review of the handling of the crisis, the House of Commons Treasury Committee made a number of specific observations about those failings:

- There were clear warning signals about the risks associated with Northern Rock's business model, both from its rapid growth as a company and from the falls in its share price from February 2007 onwards. However, although the FSA took "greater regulatory engagement" with Northern Rock, this failed to tackle the fundamental weakness in its funding model.

- The Basel II waiver, and the dividend increase this allowed to Northern Rock, came at exactly the wrong moment, and it was wrong of the FSA to allow Northern Rock to weaken its balance sheet at a time when the FSA was itself concerned about problems of liquidity that could affect the financial sector.

- The FSA did not supervise Northern Rock properly and its procedures were inadequate to supervise a bank whose business had grown so rapidly. It also appeared to be under-resourced.

- The current regulatory regime for liquidity of United Kingdom banks is flawed and requires urgent review.

- If the FSA was "very unhappy" with the stress-testing conducted by Northern Rock it appears to have failed to convey the strength of its concerns to the board of Northern Rock to secure remedial action.

- The FSA should have been more concerned about the fact that the two main appointments (the chairman and chief executive) to such a "high impact" financial institution did not possess any relevant financial qualifications.

These are clearly significant failings. I can only draw the conclusion that, as blameworthy as the management of Northern

Rock might be for its ultimate downfall, the mistakes that were made in the lead up to the crisis might have been avoided if more effective regulation had been put into place by the FSA.

Cause 4 – The handling of the crisis by the Tripartite authorities

Despite the risks attached to Northern Rock's business model, the lack of control by its regulatory body, and the high level of growth, disaster could still have been avoided had the handling of the crisis by the authorities been managed better.

On 3rd August 2007, the German government organised a £2.5 billion rescue for IKB Deutsche Industriebank, which had revealed it held massive amounts of securitised US sub-prime mortgages on its books. There was no run on that bank.

On 9th August 2007, France's biggest bank, BNP Paribas, announced it was freezing three investment funds because it could not value them. Following this, inter-bank lending pretty much ground to a halt and eventually froze. Northern Rock, at this stage, was potentially in big trouble because if the freeze continued for an extended period it would run out of cash.

About that time, the European Central Bank decided to offer unlimited funds to Eurozone banks in an effort to stabilise the banking system. In 45 minutes it doled out £60 billion in overnight loans to banks, accepting residential mortgage packages as collateral. But Northern Rock could not access this funding because it did not operate in the Eurozone.

When it became clear that Northern Rock was quickly running out of money, the Tripartite Committee (made up of representatives from the Bank of England, the FSA and the Treasury), chaired by Alistair Darling, started to look for a buyer for the bank. It transpired that Lloyds TSB was interested in acquiring Northern Rock, but only if the Bank of England provided a loan facility for £30 billion for two years to cover the risk of taking Northern Rock's business onto its balance sheet.

Reports say that the Tripartite was split on what to do.

The FSA was keen to support the takeover. But the Governor of the Bank of England did not see it as being the role of a central bank – and certainly not to the tune of £30 billion. Alistair Darling supported this decision, but many have speculated that this was more for political reasons (in that alienating the Governor of the Bank of England might cause untold political damage).

This left the board of Northern Rock with no alternative but to seek an emergency funding line from the Bank of England which, initially, was a contingency facility of £2.3 billion. Unlike the European Central Bank, which had provided emergency support to a number of European banks on an undisclosed basis, the Bank of England felt it was obliged to operate on a transparent basis. So it was planned that an announcement would be made on Monday 17th September in a carefully worded statement – which would have been designed to reassure investors and depositors.

Sadly, the news of the emergency support was leaked to the BBC on the evening of 13th September, leading to large queues forming outside Northern Rock branches early on Friday 14th September. The run continued until the following Tuesday when, finally, an announcement was made by Alistair Darling that the government would fully guarantee all deposits.

In the event, and with the benefit of hindsight, had the Bank of England supported the Lloyds TSB proposed takeover, the end result would have been considerably better all round than that which eventually occurred. The company would have been saved, jobs would have been saved, the run would not have occurred and the brand would have remained intact. We will never know if the takeover would have happened because discussions had only reached a very early stage.

Why did the Bank of England not provide support to Northern Rock when the crisis occurred, quickly, covertly and without fuss?

It is clear from the BBC Radio 4 interview with Mervyn King that he regarded the way in which Northern Rock had conducted its business as reckless. That being the case, he felt that supporting such banks created a moral hazard because other banks, which had perhaps operated their businesses on a more prudent basis, might regard that as encouraging banks to take risks.

Whilst I can understand the moral hazard argument, there was a view that the Federal Reserve Bank in the US and the European Central Bank had both taken a rather more pragmatic view in similar circumstances, and provided struggling banks with the necessary support to see them through their difficulties. That involved lending against a wide range of collateral (including relatively illiquid assets). The reason was that this particular crisis was unusually severe and failure to handle it successfully could potentially put the whole financial system into jeopardy – this has been described as the risk of contagion.

The Northern Rock run highlighted the fact that the Tripartite, as a regulatory system to control the financial stability, had comprehensively failed on the first occasion it had been tested. That was partly because it was unclear who would take the lead role in the event of such a crisis, and partly because there was not complete agreement between the three parties as to how the situation should best be handled.

The Treasury Committee review in January 2008 supported this view. Whilst it did not see the need to dismantle the Tripartite framework, it did see the need for it to be reviewed. As part of this review it recommended that consideration should be given to the appointment of a new position, "Deputy Governor of the Bank of England and Head of Financial Stability", and that person would assume direct responsibility for the exercise of powers relating to the handling of failing banks.

One of the more interesting conclusions from the Treasury report reviewing how failing banks in the UK should be dealt with, was that banks are "special" and part of the fabric of society. Whilst banks should be allowed to fail they should do so in an orderly manner and in a way that leaves the consumer fully protected.

What is obvious to me was the fact that because there had not been a banking crisis for many years, the Tripartite (which was set up by Gordon Brown in 1997) had never been tested. As a result, when the Northern Rock crisis did occur, the authorities were not prepared for it. Given that Northern Rock's problems came to the attention of the Tripartite as early as the 10th August, that suggests that they had plenty of time to get the crisis resolved without a run on the bank taking place.

An interesting comparison was how the failure of Bear Stearns bank in America was handled by the US government in March 2008. As a result of enormous sub-prime losses it got into severe difficulties, and a swift and efficient takeover of the bank by JPMorgan Chase was orchestrated by the Federal Reserve over a weekend. There was no drama and no run. Whilst shareholders had to take hefty losses, depositors' money was safe.

Most people who worked for Northern Rock at the time were of the view that the company was hung out to dry – that was how it felt. When the run was happening, nobody from within the Tripartite was prepared to make a statement to reassure the public, and the run was allowed to continue for days without any meaningful reassurance being given to depositors.

I am fairly convinced that had the Northern Rock crisis occurred in the US, or in almost any other European country, a rescue would have been facilitated behind closed doors – not with the full glare of publicity which precipitated Northern Rock's downfall.

The media coverage at the time effectively whipped up a feeling of panic. I am sure that this contributed towards the run. However, the media can only report on what information is out in the open, and it was the fact that the full extent of Northern Rock's difficulties were allowed to get in the public domain in such a high-profile way that really sealed its fate.

As events have subsequently unfolded I think that the authorities have now recognised that public confidence in the banking system in the UK, as one of the key financial centres in the world, is absolutely vital. That might mean providing support to an ailing bank, but it is a price worth paying to maintain the financial stability of the banking system. If the Northern Rock crisis has achieved anything it is to change the approach to be taken should another bank rescue be necessary in the future.

Conclusion

Northern Rock's 2007 annual report reveals the extent of the damage done following the September run, with a reported loss of £167 million for the year and a reduction of £12.1 billion in its deposits from 2006.

As I write now, Northern Rock is in the financial equivalent of intensive care. It may be a long time, if ever, before it returns to being, once again, a healthy and profitable company.

However, all is not lost. A recent bond offer by Northern Rock was oversubscribed and Andy Kuipers, the new chief executive, said:

> It proves the brand is still alive. It's been damaged but we can bring it back. The amazing thing of this whole process, with all the media speculation and criticism, is how well the business has held up. Put simply we are here to fight back and this is what will happen.

I too hope that Northern Rock lives to fight another day – the business and the people of the north-east deserve it.

Appendices

Timeline

1850

The first meeting of the Northern Counties Permanent Benefit Building and Investment Society takes place. It is held at Mr Wilcke's temperance hotel in the Royal Arcade, Pilgrim Street in the centre of Newcastle.

1865

The Rock Building Society holds its first meeting at Mr Bell's, a temperance hotel in West Clayton Street, Newcastle.

1866

Overend, Gurney & Company, known as "the banker's bank", goes into liquidation bringing down with it nearly 300 companies, including other banks who also failed. Panic ensues and crowds of depositors queue outside the bank's offices at 65 Lombard Street, London to withdraw their money.

July 1964

The Times announces the proposed £60 million merger of the Northern Counties Permanent and Rock Building Societies into the Northern Rock Building Society.

1 July 1965

The merger of the two building societies formally takes place and the Northern Rock Building Society is born. Robert Mould-Graham, ex-chairman of Northern Counties Permanent, becomes Northern Rock's first chairman.

1 October 1994

Northern Rock takes over the North of England Building Society to become a top ten player with assets exceeding £10 billion.

3 April 1996

Northern Rock Building Society announces its intention to convert to a PLC having had its demutualisation proposals approved by the board.

1 October 1997

Following 18 months of negotiations, Northern Rock Building Society converts to Northern Rock PLC. As part of the conversion, the Northern Rock Foundation is set up, which is a charitable organisation committed largely to the north-east's regional and social needs. Under the terms of the conversion, the Foundation receives 5% of the company's annual profits and 15% of shareholder voting rights.

January 1999

Northern Rock joins the FTSE100 index.

March 2001

Adam Applegarth succeeds Leo Finn as Chief Executive of Northern Rock PLC at the age of 39, having been with the company since he joined it in 1982 as an executive trainee. He quickly rose up though the ranks to become marketing director in 1990, and, in 1996, he was promoted to the board with responsibility for marketing, loans and information technology.

6 April 2003

Northern Rock takes over from NTL as sponsors of premiership football club Newcastle United in a two-year deal.

20 April 2004

Northern Rock announces an extension to its sponsorship of Newcastle United in a new £25 million five-year deal for five seasons from 2005/6 up to 2009/10. Adam Applegarth says: "We continue to see this as a long-term relationship as the Newcastle United brand is being enhanced both on and off the pitch."

24 January 2007

Northern Rock's 2006 year-end results announced. Another record year with assets increasing by 24% to over £100 billion for the first time and profit growth increased by 19%. Northern Rock becomes the fifth largest mortgage lender in the UK. Its market share of new mortgages rises from 7% in 2005, to 13% in 2006. Adam Applegarth announces the bank's aim to become a "top 3" mortgage lender.

2 April 2007

Northern Rock issues a positive interim trading statement indicating a 34% increase in total net lending against the same period in 2006. The statement also mentions the launch in February 2007 of its retail deposit arm in Denmark with a view to broadening its deposit base. There is mention of the proposed sale of its commercial lending book to improve its capital efficiency.

Adam Applegarth says: "We have started 2007 strongly, with lending performance well ahead of the comparable period last year and a strong pipeline of business to deliver asset growth in the top half of our strategic range."

25 July 2007

Northern Rock issues a set of positive trading results, having sold mortgages worth a record £10.7 billion in the first half of 2007, with residential mortgage net lending up 57% on the same period the previous year. During this period, Northern Rock sold approximately one out of every five mortgages granted in the UK. However, profits, despite being up 26.6%, have been squeezed as a result of more expensive money market borrowing rates. Total assets have grown 28% to £113 billion, its new residential lending remains "low risk" and sales growth from its core mortgage business remains good.

9 August 2007

The date the credit crunch officially started. French bank BNP Paribas's decision to suspend three of its investment funds which were exposed to the US sub-prime market creates a shock to the global financial system, causing the money markets to freeze.

This date heralded the start of Northern Rock's problems.

13 August 2007

Following initial contact from the FSA on the previous working day regarding the impact of the freezing of the money markets on Northern Rock, the board responds to confirm that it would face potential difficulties if the market freeze continued. Thereafter, the FSA and Northern Rock are in twice daily telephone contact.

14 August 2007

First discussions on Northern Rock take place between the Tripartite authorities.

The Governor of the Bank of England is alerted of a potential problem.

16 August 2007

Dr Matt Ridley, Chairman of Northern Rock, speaks directly with the Governor of the Bank of England by telephone, and the possibility of a support operation is discussed.

During the course of the next few weeks, Northern Rock and the Tripartite authorities pursue a threefold strategy to extricate the bank from its difficulties, i.e. trying to raise capital in the markets, trying to find a safe haven and, in the event that these are not successful, receiving a support facility from the Bank of England guaranteed by the government.

4 September 2007

LIBOR rises to almost 6.8%, its highest level in nearly nine years. This is a full percentage point above the Bank of England base rate, which is 5.75%.

12 September 2007

The Bank of England reacts to the financial banking crisis by announcing that it would be prepared to issue emergency loans to any bank that experienced temporary difficulties as a consequence of the current difficulties in the financial markets.

Whilst the ECB and Federal Reserve Bank had pumped significant funds into the European and US financial markets, this lead has not yet been followed by the UK.

13 September 2007

News is leaked that Northern Rock has sought emergency funding from the Bank of England in its capacity as lender of the last resort.

The announcement catches both Northern Rock and the authorities off guard, and previous plans to formally announce the position on the following Monday are overtaken by events.

Whilst an announcement by the BBC the same evening does not suggest that Northern Rock is in danger of going bust, the impact on the bank's depositors is immense.

14 September 2007

Long queues form outside Northern Rock's branches following the previous day's news announcement.

Despite attempts by Northern Rock and the government to reassure investors the panic continues. Northern Rock's shares fall sharply by a further 32%.

Angry investors trying to withdraw their savings online complain that the website is not functioning, leading to fears that the bank is deliberately preventing investors from withdrawing their savings.

Pictures of the run on Northern Rock, the first on any UK bank in 141 years, are beamed all over the world.

15 September 2007

There is no let up to the queues over the weekend, and despite a television appearance by Adam Applegarth there is no other announcement by any of the government authorities.

Speculation emerges that at least £4 billion in deposits has been withdrawn from Northern Rock in just two days. The website is now functioning properly after initially being jammed by the sheer volume of traffic.

The crisis continues.

17 September 2007

Once again there is no sign of any let up as the queues continue. No announcement is made during the day by the authorities, and commentators show concern about the risk of contagion and the potential of the run spreading to other banks. The share price falls again by a further 40%, down 80% from its 2007 peak of £12.50.

Finally, in the evening the Chancellor, Alistair Darling, announces that the government will guarantee all existing deposits held with Northern Rock to the level of 100%.

18 September 2007

The queues finally stop, following yesterday's announcement. However, Northern Rock's brand is already being described as "irreversibly damaged" and it seems increasingly likely that either a break up of the company or a takeover by another bank is a serious possibility.

19 September 2007

As a direct result of the Northern Rock crisis, Mervyn King, Governor of the Bank of England, announces that £10 billion is to be injected into the UK financial markets in an effort to stabilise the situation and reduce the risk of damage to the economy.

20 September 2007

The new depositor guarantee arrangements announced by the Chancellor on 18th September are confirmed by the Treasury and relate to existing depositors with Northern Rock as at midnight on 19th September. New deposits are not covered 100%, instead existing rules apply – 100% guarantee for the first £2,000, 90% guarantee for the next £33,000.

23 September 2007

It is reported that at least a dozen of the biggest financial institutions in Britain and Europe have snubbed pleas to rescue Northern Rock, including HSBC, Barclays, Lloyds TSB, RBS, Santander and Crédit Agricole.

25 September 2007

After considerable media pressure, Northern Rock announces that it is cancelling the dividend that it was due to pay shareholders in October, which would have cost the bank £59 million. This was following a statement from the company just a few days earlier that it still planned to pay the dividend.

26 September 2007

The head of the CBI, Richard Lambert, says that the near collapse of Northern Rock revealed deep flaws in Britain's Tripartite system of financial regulation. In contrast to government ministers and regulators who have defended the combined efforts of the FSA, the Bank of England and the Treasury, he says that the system had "been found wanting under fire".

3 October 2007

Angela Knight, chief executive of the British Bankers' Association, launches a fierce attack on the industry's regulators for their handling of the Northern Rock crisis and criticises the FSA for failing to spot the dangers of liquidity risk.

9 October 2007

The 100% guarantee given by the Treasury to Northern Rock's existing depositors is extended to include new deposits with Northern Rock. Meanwhile, Hector Sants, Chief Executive of the FSA, appears before the Treasury Select Committee, which is enquiring into the role of the regulatory body in the run up to the crisis. He admits that there were lessons to be learned from the way in which Northern Rock had been regulated.

10 October 2007

Shares in Northern Rock surge 34% to their highest for three weeks as controversial hedge fund manager Jon Wood of J.C. Flowers reveals that he has taken his stake in the bailed-out building society-turned-bank to more than 4%.

12 October 2007

The Virgin Group, led by Sir Richard Branson, emerges as a surprise contender for the takeover of Northern Rock.

The proposal is for Virgin to inject equity into the business and rebrand it as "Virgin Money". Jayne-Anne Gadhia, Virgin Money's CEO, is being lined up to take charge if the bid is successful.

16 October 2007

Key members of Northern Rock's board attend a Treasury Select Committee Hearing to face questions from MPs relating to their roles in the lead up to the run on Northern Rock. The Committee is highly critical of the company's "reckless lending activity" in the run up to the crash.

19 October 2007

Dr Ridley resigns, three days after he was accused by the Treasury Select Committee of clinging onto office. Ridley's departure was considered inevitable after his woeful performance in front of the recent hearing.

Bryan Sanderson is appointed the new chairman of Northern Rock.

2 November 2007

Bryan Sanderson authorises the bank to send out information packs to any potential bidders and warns that it is unlikely that any future sale could go ahead without some reduction to the 5,700 workforce employed across the region. He also says that Northern Rock could be more than £25 billion in debt by the time the government aid dries up in February.

4 November 2007

Northern Rock gives a two week deadline to potential bidders to make a formal offer for its assets. It has sent out a formal memorandum to potential bidders and is looking at running a restructuring and sale process in tandem in an effort to attract wider bid interest.

Northern Rock savers have now withdrawn a reported £14 billion in deposits from the bank. The figure, thought to have emerged during due diligence by three possible bidders, equates to almost 60% of the total £24 billion in deposits held at the bank before it was forced to go to the Bank of England for emergency funding. Close to £3 billion was withdrawn in the three-day run on the bank in mid September.

So far, Northern Rock has borrowed £22.8 billion from the Bank of England to pay withdrawals and fund lending. This could rise to close to £30 billion by the end of the year.

9 November 2007

Sir Richard Branson, says the consortium put together for the acquisition of Northern Rock will surprise critics who have discounted his chances of successfully acquiring the company. Virgin has put together a heavyweight consortium of investors including US insurer AIG, private equity firm W.L. Ross, London based hedge fund Toscafund, and Hong Kong based First Eastern Investment Group.

11 November 2007

It is reported that Luqman Arnold, one of the City's most experienced bankers, has secretly assembled a crack team to rescue Northern Rock. Arnold, who was instrumental in turning around Abbey National, is proposing a salvage plan which will not involve a sale or break up of the company. It is expected that full details of the bid will be presented to Northern Rock's board prior to the November 16 deadline.

15 November 2007

Stories emerge in the newspapers that Adam Applegarth sold shares valued at £2.6 million in two large transactions in August 2006 and January 2007 (when shares were sold at £11.98). Shares closed the previous day at £1.39.

16 November 2007

Northern Rock announces that chief executive Adam Applegarth has resigned from his position, although it is intended that he be kept on until January 2008 to assist with the second phase of the bank's strategic review. Opposition MPs welcomed the news, but argued that the decision to keep Applegarth on the board was misguided.

His board colleagues David Baker, Chief Operating Officer, Keith Currie, Treasurer, and Andy Kuipers, Marketing Director, also stand down, but remain officers of the bank and will continue to have responsibility for their full range of duties. Dave Jones continues to serve on the board as Finance Director. The four other directors to resign are Sir Derek Wanless, Nichola Pease, Adam Fenwick and Rosemary Radcliffe. They will retire as non-executive directors with immediate effect.

The outgoing non-execs are replaced by John Devaney, who is chairman of National Air Traffic Services, and Simon Laffin, a private equity expert who is currently an advisor to CVC Capital Partners and was previously the chief financial officer of the supermarket chain, Safeway.

18 November 2007

Northern Rock's advisors (Merrill Lynch, Citigroup and Blackstone) are this weekend considering initial proposals for full or partial takeovers. Bids have been received from Virgin Group, Olivant, and US private equity firm, Cerberus. The deadline, however, is flexible and private equity group J.C. Flowers has been given room to submit its bid next week.

19 November 2007

Northern Rock says that bids received so far from potential investors are "materially below" its share price.

Two suitors, Virgin Group and Olivant, have both submitted proposals to rescue the firm. It expects to receive further expressions of interest over the next few days.

21 November 2007

The latest bidder for Northern Rock, US private equity group J.C. Flowers, puts forward proposals that would leave shareholders with next to nothing. Sources say that Flowers plans to pay £15 billion of the Bank of England's £24 billion loan immediately and the remaining £9 billion by the end of 2010.

Northern Rock's shares hit a new low of 60p before recovering to close at 97p.

24 November 2007

FSA Chairman, Sir Callum McCarthy, admits the watchdog had not paid enough attention to off balance sheet assets prior to the credit crunch and describes the Northern Rock debacle as "deeply sobering". McCarthy plans deeper scrutiny of all banks and their investments in obscure debt securities such as SIVs and CDOs.

25 November 2007

Northern Rock's largest shareholder issues a warning over plans to sell off the troubled bank. The chief executive of RAB Capital, Philip Richards, said he would vote against a proposed takeover of the bank that did not properly value its shares. The board of Northern Rock is continuing to assess a total of 10 bids for the bank.

26 November 2007

Northern Rock's board confirms to the Stock Exchange that the strategic review has been concluded and the Virgin consortium is the preferred bidder for Northern Rock. It is intended to take forward discussions on an accelerated basis with Virgin.

It is also confirmed that the UK Treasury has extended its guarantee arrangements to depositors until the authorities can satisfy themselves that the current financial market instability is over and the position of depositors protected.

28 November 2007

It is reported that hedge fund SRM Global snapped up 6.97m of Northern Rock shares yesterday to become its biggest investor. SRM Global has said that the auction of the company should be halted as it could lead to the group being sold off too cheaply.

Virgin still remains the preferred bidder. It has emerged that if the Virgin bid is successful Northern Rock would have to pay a license fee for use of the Virgin name. This would fluctuate depending on profitability.

30 November 2007

A four-way bidding war is developing to acquire Northern Rock, with J.C. Flowers, former Abbey boss Luqman Arnold, and private equity firm Cerberus all poised to make improved bids in comparison to Virgin who currently have "preferred bidder" status.

Shares recover from earlier losses to close ahead at 118p.

4 December 2007

Reports emerge that the Virgin Group may struggle to finance its preferred bid as it appears that Deutsche Bank may not be able to raise sufficient capital and therefore would have to withdraw from the consortium of funders. Other potential bidders at this stage still include Olivant (Luqman Arnold), J.C. Flowers and Cerberus.

Shares drop to 109p.

5 December 2007

The *Financial Times* reports that banks will today call for a full and independent enquiry into the near collapse of Northern Rock. The British Bankers' Association will urge ministers to build on the investigation being conducted by the Treasury Select Committee by setting up an urgent independent enquiry into how and why the authorities failed to prevent the run on the bank. The industry body said it was worried that Mr Darling was consulting on regulatory changes without an adequate evidence base.

6 December 2007

Since the run on Northern Rock in September it is estimated that the bank's retail deposit base has dropped by over half – from approximately £25 billion at its peak to about £11 billion now.

It is understood that Virgin, if successful, expects to increase deposits up to £30 billion over the next five years.

7 December 2007

J.C. Flowers withdraws from the auction to buy Northern Rock as it had found it "impossible" to construct a deal that would deliver the required value for Northern Rock shareholders alongside its own profitability criteria.

Olivant makes a long-awaited proposal for Northern Rock. Its proposal would enable Northern Rock to quickly repay between £10 billion and £15 billion of Bank of England loans, aiming to repay the loans in full by the end of 2009. Olivant's trump card is that it has considerable shareholder support behind its bid (in particular RAB Capital and SRM Global). However, a disadvantage is that it would be stuck with the now discredited Northern Rock brand.

9 December 2007

Fresh doubts have been cast on Northern Rock's future, with Liberal Democrat leader Vince Cable saying plans to sell the troubled bank "will not work". The global credit crisis has meant that no bidder could raise the money needed to pay back the £25 billion in government loans made to the bank, he told the BBC.

Northern Rock's board say they want to spend the next month working with both Virgin and Olivant to refine their bids, making it extremely unlikely that any deal would be reached by the Christmas deadline set by the government.

12 December 2007

Olivant is threatening to abandon its attempted rescue of Northern Rock, accusing it of frustrating its attempts to negotiate a massive line of credit with Citigroup and Deutsche Bank. There is serious concern that if Olivant pulls out that will leave the way clear for Virgin to make an unopposed bid for the bank.

13 December 2007

Adam Applegarth announces that he is leaving Northern Rock with immediate effect. Andy Kuipers, previously removed from the board, is appointed in his place.

Northern Rock is ejected from the FTSE100 index, having joined it in September 2001. Once commanding a market value of £5.3 billion, it is now worth an estimated £417 million.

14 December 2007

Northern Rock persuades Olivant to remain in the running to take control of the bank, and announces that Olivant will be given joint preferred-bidder status and equal access to the books as Virgin.

16 December 2007

It is understood that the government, the Bank of England and the Northern Rock board believe that Olivant's plans do not include enough new equity – and this could undermine the future financial strength of the bank.

SRM's Jon Wood is understood to have received legal advice indicating that the government would need to pay no less than £4.10 per share, equivalent to Northern Rock's book value. The shares are currently trading at around 90p.

21 December 2007

Northern Rock confirms that an emergency meeting for shareholders will be held on 15th January to discuss its sale process. The meeting will be the first high-profile public debate on the Northern Rock situation, and an opportunity for shareholders to have their say.

RAB Capital and SRM Global, two of the bank's major shareholders, are calling for restrictions on the board's ability to sell the company's assets or issue new shares.

8 January 2008

One of Northern Rock's largest shareholders, SRM Global, is putting pressure on Alistair Darling not to nationalise Northern Rock. It is also threatening the government with legal action through the European Court of Human Rights should the shareholders not be offered a fair price for their shares in compensation should the company ultimately be nationalised.

11 January 2008

It is announced that Northern Rock has raised £2.25 billion by selling its "Lifetime" portfolio of equity release mortgages to the investment bank JPMorgan. The sale proceeds are to be used to reduce the Bank of England loan, which is said to be standing at £26 billion.

This is the first occasion that Northern Rock has been able to raise any funds from the investment markets since before the run. This portfolio of mortgages, however, is said to be of particularly high quality.

Reports also emerge that Northern Rock's pension fund is £100 million in deficit. These will be of particular concern to any potential buyers of the bank who will need to fund the shortfall.

15 January 2008

A shareholders meeting instigated by RAB Capital and SRM Global takes place at Newcastle Arena and is attended by just 600 Northern Rock shareholders, who vote on proposals put forward by Northern Rock that would effectively stop the bank from negotiating a sale without shareholder consent.

Northern Rock chairman, Bryan Sanderson, has to deal with a number of awkward questions from angry shareholders.

Only one proposal in the ultimate vote is carried and this has limited impact on the management's powers.

19 January 2008

The government makes it clear that, whilst it is still pursuing a private sale of Northern Rock, nationalisation is still a real option. Within the last few days it has also been announced that Ron Sandler will take control of Northern Rock in the event of its nationalisation.

21 January 2008

The chances of a private sale appear to have increased as Alistair Darling announces a plan, devised by its advisors, Goldman Sachs, to convert Northern Rock's £25 billion Bank of England loan into bonds so that they can be sold to investors.

The move is designed to facilitate Northern Rock's sale and potential bidders have until the 4th February to submit their revised proposals.

26 January 2008

The House of Commons Treasury Committee publishes its detailed report entitled "The run on the Rock", which investigates the background to, and the causes of, the September run and the effective failure of Northern Rock. Amongst the key findings are that the FSA was guilty of a "systematic failure of duty" over the Northern Rock crisis.

MPs call for the Bank of England to set up a new position, Head of Financial Stability, within the Tripartite in an effort to clarify areas of specific responsibility should a similar bank crisis occur in the future.

4 February 2008

Olivant pull out of the bidding process leaving Virgin and Northern Rock's "in-house proposal" the only remaining two bidders.

6 February 2008

It emerges that Virgin Group's plans for Northern Rock – if it is successful – will involve up to 1,000 job cuts. This is to meet the government's target of three years to achieve repayment of the Bank of England loan.

12 February 2008

The Virgin-led consortium is advised by the Treasury that it remains its preferred bidder and is therefore still the favourite to take over Northern Rock. However, the Group is asked to improve the terms of its rescue plan. The Treasury wants Virgin to offer more for the billions of pounds of financial support being provided by the government and a bigger potential stake in Northern Rock for the taxpayer.

The in-house rescue plan is also being revisited with a view to producing a more acceptable outcome.

17 February 2008

News breaks on Sky TV over the weekend that Northern Rock is to be nationalised.

Chancellor Alistair Darling says that neither the Virgin nor the in-house proposal had proved to be acceptable and from the various choices available it had been decided that a temporary period of public ownership is likely to offer the best protection for savers and taxpayers.

Ron Sandler is confirmed as the executive chairman of Northern Rock and given the responsibility of running the bank through its period of public ownership.

18 February 2008

Shares in Northern Rock are suspended.

Alistair Darling says the nationalised bank will operate "at arm's length" from the government and says the bill to begin the nationalisation process will be launched in parliament on Tuesday.

21 February 2008

After three days debate in both the House of Commons and the House of Lords, the bill to nationalise Northern Rock is approved.

Ron Sandler announces that the controversial "Together" mortgage product has been axed.

10 March 2008

Most of the officials at the FSA who were directly responsible for the flawed supervision of Northern Rock have resigned. Of the seven FSA supervisors working closely on the bank before its implosion last year five have left, the FSA has admitted.

17 March 2008

The government presents its initial outline of its rescue plan for Northern Rock to the European Commission who need to give the proposal its approval under European legislation.

18 March 2008

Northern Rock announces it will focus on growing its deposits whilst shrinking its mortgage book. Its competitors are concerned that Northern Rock is breaching unfair competition rules by offering attractive deposit rates as a result of having financial support from the Bank of England.

Meanwhile, it is clear that plans to shrink its mortgage book by roughly half will potentially involve some 2,000 job cuts.

26 March 2008

The FSA confirms that it will be overhauling its procedures as a result of the weaknesses identified in its handling of the Northern Rock crisis. It admits that too few regulators were given the responsibility of overseeing Northern Rock and that it was not monitored closely enough.

31 March 2008

Northern Rock's financial year-end accounts to 31st December 2007 are finally published. They reveal that the bank made losses of £168 million in the financial year after £422 milliom in write downs.

Ron Sandler, government appointed chairman, sets out detailed plans to return it to breakeven within three years. The mortgage book would reduce from £107 billion to £50 billion by 2011. Between £25 billion and £30 billion of mortgages due for review in 2008 would automatically move to higher interest rates, leading them to move to other lenders. Unsecured and commercial lending will cease. Costs will be cut by 20%, with staff reductions of up to 2,000 to be achieved by 2011. He also said he planned for Northern Rock to have repaid the Bank of England loans by 2010. The accounts also confirm that deposits had fallen by £12.1 billion since 31st December 2006.

3 April 2008

The European Commission opens an investigation into the government's plans to restructure Northern Rock to ensure that its proposals will not distort the market. The enquiry is designed to establish whether the plans comply with the European Union's rules on state aid and does not give the bank an unfair competitive advantage over its rivals.

4 April 2008

Reports emerge that Northern Rock's shareholders are set to apply for a judicial review of the government's decision to nationalise the bank. "The biggest bank robbery in history," says Sunderland-born Dennis Grainger, who is spearheading the UK Shareholders' Association (UKSA) campaign on behalf of small shareholders in the north-east.

The group says the government has "rigged" the system it set up to rule on how much compensation shareholders should receive. The valuation will be based on a number of assumptions about the bank, including that it is in administration and unable to continue as a going concern, neither of which was true at the time of nationalisation, claims the association.

Chart of Northern Rock's Share Price

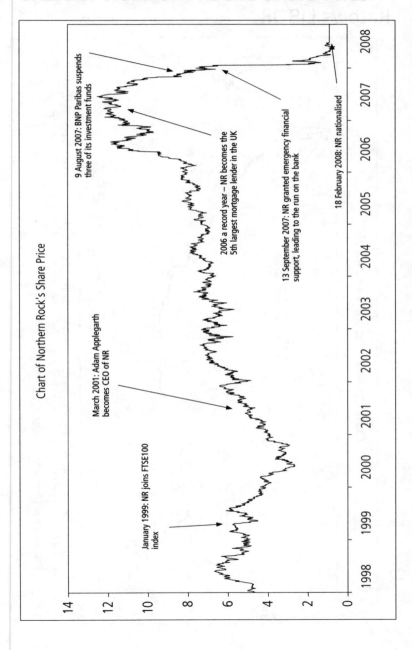

Chart of Northern Rock's Share Price

January 1999: NR joins FTSE100 index

March 2001: Adam Applegarth becomes CEO of NR

9 August 2007: BNP Paribas suspends three of its investment funds

2006 a record year – NR becomes the 5th largest mortgage lender in the UK

13 September 2007: NR granted emergency financial support, leading to the run on the bank

18 February 2008: NR nationalised

Chart of the Bank of England Base Rate vs LIBOR

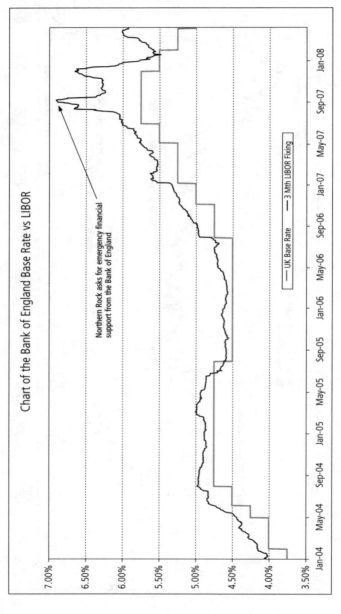

Chart of the Bank of England Base Rate vs LIBOR

Northern Rock asks for emergency financial support from the Bank of England

— UK Base Rate   — 3 Mth LIBOR Fixing

Source: J.C. Rathbone Associates Limited (www.jcra.co.uk)

Index

Royal Bank of Scotland 77,
105
SRM Global Investments 103,
106, 108
Treasury, the 54, 60
Treasury Select Committee 69,
83, 94, 127-128, 130, 133
Tripartite Standing Committee
53-54, 61, 70, 131-134
Unite 96
Virgin Group 80, 96, 101-
104, 109, 112, 120, 123
Workington Permanent
Building Society 5

People

Applegarth, Adam 3, 7, 23,
27, 33, 41, 44-45, 65-66, 74,
78, 83-89, 95-96, 98-99, 105,
128
Arnold, Luqman (see also
'Olivant') 98, 104
Ashby, Robin 123
Branson, Sir Richard (see also
'Virgin Group') 93, 104, 123
Brown, Gordon 123-124, 134
Cable, Vince 63
Darling, Alistair 54, 64, 66,
70, 94-95, 98, 109, 117, 124,
131-132
Devaney, John 99
Dickinson, Robert 6
Fallon, Michael MP 94

Fenwick, Adam 99
Finn, Leo 7, 24
Gadhia, Jayne-Anne 104
Gibson, Sir Ian 83
Gieve, Sir John 54
King, Mervyn 54, 57, 69, 71,
98, 132-133
Knight, Angela 122
Kuipers, Andy 105-107, 135
Lambert, Richard 78
Laffin, Simon 99
McCarthy, Sir Callum 54, 94
Osborne, George MP 123
Pease, Nichola 99
Peston, Robert 60
Radcliffe, Rosemary 99
Ridley, Dr Matt 54, 77, 83-85,
88, 90
Robson, Bobby 75
Sanderson, Bryan 95, 107
Sandler, Ron 118, 121
Sants, Hector 54, 94
Sharp, Chris 6-7
Thurso, John 86
Wanless, Sir Derek 83, 85-86,
99